The Missing Ministry

Safety, Risk Management, and Protecting Your Church

The GuideOne Center for Risk Management

Loveland, Colorado
www.group.com

The Missing Ministry
Safety, Risk Management, and Protecting Your Church

Unless otherwise noted, Scripture taken from the HOLY BIBLE, NEW INTERNATIONAL VERSION®. Copyright © 1973, 1978, 1984 by International Bible Society. Used by permission of Zondervan Publishing House. All rights reserved.

This book is designed to provide accurate and authoritative information in regard to the subject matter covered. It is provided with the understanding that the authors and publishers are not engaged in rendering legal, accounting, or other professional service. If legal advice or other expert assistance is required, the services of a competent professional should be sought.

Please note that all of the stories about churches in this book are based on actual events, actions, and incidents. However, the names of some churches and individuals involved have been changed in order to protect their privacy.

Credits
Editors: Craig A. Bubeck and Candace McMahan
Developer: Roxanne Wieman
Chief Creative Officer: Joani Schultz
Copy Editor: Daniel Birks
Art Director/Designer: Jeff A. Storm
Print Production Artist: Coffee Bean Design Company
Cover Designer: Thomas Patrick
Production Manager: DeAnne Lear

Library of Congress Cataloging-in-Publication Data

The missing ministry : safety, risk management, and protecting your church / The GuideOne Center for Risk Management.
    p. cm.
  ISBN-13: 978-0-7644-3679-6 (pbk. : alk. paper)
  1. Church management. 2. Corporations, Religious--Safety measures. 3. Church buildings--Security measures. 4. Church buildings--Safety measures. I. GuideOne Center for Risk Management.
  BV652.9.M57 2008
  254--dc22
                                    2008013852

10 9 8 7 6 5 4 3 2 1   17 16 15 14 13 12 11 10 09 08

Printed in the United States of America.

Table of Contents

Chapter 1

Shepherd-Protector: The High Calling

They Never Thought It Would Happen to Them

Pastor John could only stare at the attorney's letter in his trembling hand—he could hardly make out the words on the page, and with each sentence, he kept looking up from the letter to the office staff around him. Susan was trying to hold back her tears, Jim just kept staring at the floor, and Bill sat at a desk, his head lowered in his hands.

It couldn't be—the pain from last month's tragic accident was still heavy in their hearts. The church's van had drifted onto the shoulder of the road, the driver overcorrected, lost control, and the van flipped over several times. Two of their youth were lost—14-year-old Michael Borden was pronounced dead at the scene, and Susan Miller slipped away in the ICU the next morning. Michael's older sister had started physical therapy, and last Sunday the entire congregation prayed again for young Joe Adams, who was finally in stable condition. The other three injured passengers were well enough to attend the service, and it seemed that maybe their gradual recovery could lead the way to the church's healing. But the victims' families would never be the same.

Now this—this letter was like salt in their wounds, adding insult to injury.

His eyes couldn't get past one phrase about a third of the way down—he kept reading it over and over again: "…seeking damages of $8 million." They were alleging the van was unsafe and had been operated by an unqualified driver.

Don couldn't help but flash back to a little less than a year ago when he'd first received the news that he'd been voted to chair the church board. He was so happy. It was such an honor to be vested with this trust.

But now…

Don sat with the rest of the board, across the table from their attorney, Samuel Hengston. And no one in the room showed even a glimmer of hope.

"I don't understand how this could be," Don rejoined. He'd been over this from several different angles with Samuel, and now he could only be direct. "We were the ones who first discovered the abuse in our classroom. We went directly to the police and cooperated fully. Our own people testified in court against that child molester and made sure he was prosecuted."

Don could tell that Samuel was following his words attentively. But nothing Don could say seemed to have any impact. "We all feel devastated for the children who were abused and their families, but I don't see how they can blame the church for this."

Samuel looked down and continued to nod. "I know, Don."

Despair came over Don as his eyes moved around the table from one friend to another. Finally, he looked at their beloved senior pastor. Rich had remained fixed and silent. Don searched pleadingly into the eyes of his friend. "What are we going to do, Rich? Right when we've seen such incredible growth, such incredible ministry. And now this? A lawsuit for $26 million? It'll close down everything, for good. Is this what God wants?"

Pastor Rich's eyes narrowed, and he whispered almost inaudibly, "No, it isn't."

The Shepherd's Calling

Whether you're a pastor, a church administrator, board member, or some other type of church leader, you have been called by God to shepherd the church. And shepherding requires a commitment to protection. This is why we believe practicing risk management fulfills a biblical responsibility to be good shepherds of the people and property God has entrusted to the church.

Shepherding God's people is a high calling, and many individuals who have been called like to think of their work as being about benevolence, love, and growth. It's about leading a family that is welcoming and generous—a light to the world, not a dark fortress of fear and paranoia.

The Bible cautions church leaders: "Keep watch over yourselves and all the flock, of which the Holy Spirit has made you overseers. Be shepherds of the church of God" (Acts 20:28a). Later, Paul similarly writes to Timothy expressing his concern for the church, describing it as a precious charge: "Guard the good deposit that was entrusted to you" (2 Timothy 1:14a).

Shepherding the flock is about much more than security and self-preservation, to be sure (a sheep's life is about feeding, drinking, growing, even playing). But protection is still an important part of a shepherd's job description.

In whatever capacity we may serve as shepherds of our local flocks, our spiritual calling must also be concerned for the physical safety and well-being of that flock. Although it would be much easier to whistle in the dark and assume God will take up the slack where we leave off, the sobering reality is that God calls us to oversee and protect—to be shrewd in a world of wolves.

The Right Tools for the Right Job

Sadly, the two introductory stories in this chapter (based on actual events) are dramatic examples of the tragedies that hundreds of churches experience each year. But what makes many such tragic stories even more heartbreaking is that they could have been easily prevented if the churches had taken more seriously their calling as protectors of the flock.

In today's uncertain world where new and increasing dangers exist, wise shepherds of a church are called upon to implement key safety and security precautions to protect their flocks. So if you've picked up this book and are committed to becoming an even better shepherd, we commend you. There are both biblical and practical reasons for you to be concerned about the safety, security, and financial future of your church.

This is why we have created this book—to give you the shepherding tools to help your church start a program that may

- save a life;
- prevent a serious injury;
- protect a child from being sexually abused;
- avoid an accident in a church vehicle;
- safeguard your church against burglary and arson;
- stop the theft of church funds;
- protect the reputation of your church leaders;
- prevent a costly lawsuit against your church; and
- demonstrate love, care, and concern for the congregation.

While the topics in this book focus on church safety and security procedures—or what is also known as *risk management,* this is not a tedious manual filled with dry information. Rather, we intend this to be an everyday, practical guide to church safety and security that we believe you'll find interesting and beneficial.

The material contained in this book will provide you with easy and effective ways to establish a basic safety and security program using the "EFFECT" approach, which helps you identify and minimize your church's greatest areas of risk. In addition, we've also developed a *SafeChurch Resource Packet* containing a wide variety of additional tools to assist your church, including reproducible forms, checklists, further specific advice, updates, and many other essential tools—all of which you can easily download for free at the SafeChurch website: www .safechurch.com. Many of these tools are referred to directly in the book, so it's important that you download and print these crucial resources.

Naturally, reading this book does not guarantee that your church can avoid every type of problem that might arise. There are, of course, dangers and risks that are beyond anyone's control. But we think you'll be surprised at how easily and affordably you can enhance the safety and security of your church with these suggestions and tools. Even taking just a few small steps can make a huge difference.

If this information helps you prevent just one accident, injury, or other serious problem, your time reading will be well spent. And if you've ever worried about the possibility of a costly lawsuit or asked yourself, "Are we doing enough to protect our people, property, and reputation?" this book will address your concerns.

The Shepherd's Strategy—Risk Management

What is risk management all about?

Admittedly, the term can seem out of place in a church setting. Furthermore, risk management is one of those industry terms that sounds rather intimidating and complex. In truth, however, risk management is a fairly simple and straightforward concept. And since the term is commonly used by many professionals today, it's important to understand its true meaning.

By definition, risk management is the process of identifying risks (such as a fire hazard) facing an organization, and then taking steps to minimize the effects of those risks on the organization. In other words, risk management focuses on addressing problems that range from accidents and injuries to crimes and lawsuits.

There are several ways that churches can address these issues. One way is to *avoid* the risk; that is, to determine that an activity (such as skydiving) is so risky that the church will just not undertake it at all. Another way is to *control* the risk; that is, to take steps to either prevent the risk from happening or reduce the likelihood of its happening. For example, by regularly inspecting the premises, a church can help control or reduce the risk of people getting injured by falling down on the property. Another way is to *transfer* the risk; that is, to have another organization take on the risk that your church might otherwise face. For example, an insurance policy can effectively transfer the risk of a covered loss, such as a fire, from the church to its insurer up to the limits of the policy. A final way is to *retain* the risk; that is, to make a decision that your church will retain the legal and financial consequences of a risk such as a theft or liability claim. A deductible in the church's insurance policy is an example of risk retention.

Ultimately, the goal of risk management is to enhance the safety and security of your people and property.

When you hear the term *risk management,* you can think "safety and security" if you prefer. Or when discussing a risk management program at your church, you might want to call it a *safety and security program* so people will grasp the true meaning. For practical purposes, we will refer to risk management programs and safety and security programs interchangeably throughout this book.

We need to define what constitutes a basic church risk management program (or safety and security program). But as we do so, keep in mind that a risk management program does not have to be elaborate or expensive to be effective.

In general, a basic risk management program includes the following elements:

- *Church leaders* who are committed to enhancing safety and security and are willing to support a program that accomplishes those goals.
- A small group of church members who serve on a *Church Safety and Security Team* (or Risk Management Team). These individuals identify the church's greatest risks, design the program, and are dedicated to keeping it going.
- *Written policies* and procedures that address your church's greatest risks, such as transportation safety, child and youth safety, and building security.
- *Church staff and members* who follow the program's policies and procedures.
- An *ongoing effort* to make the safety and security program a key ministry within the church.

The $1 Million Question

Now that we have our terminology clarified, you need to ask yourself the $1 million question: Does your church really have a formalized risk management program in place? If yours is like most churches, the answer is no. In fact, research shows that only two churches out of five in America has any type of risk management program. That's one reason we titled this book *The Missing Ministry,* because so few churches have established safety and security programs.

Some church leaders also might think that having church insurance is the equivalent to a risk management program. But insurance is only a part of the equation. While it's critical to have insurance in place in the event of an incident at your church, insurance cannot do anything to prevent an accident from happening in the first place. That's why it's so important that your church develops a solid risk management program that includes written policies and procedures and other tools to safeguard various aspects of your ministry.

Guard Against Devastating Lawsuits

We must acknowledge one real and pragmatic reason for risk management: Without a risk management program in place, your church could easily face a $1 million lawsuit. And the cost could be even higher as jury awards, settlements, and judgment amounts continue to climb.

We're not overstating the threat. Million-dollar lawsuits against churches are beginning to happen more frequently than you might have ever imagined. Consider these recent cases:

- In New York, a jury awarded $11.45 million in damages after two teens were sexually molested by the church's youth minister.

- In Missouri, a church was sued after five young people drowned in a river during a church outing.

- In Ohio, a jury awarded $5.76 million in damages after a young boy was spanked by a teacher in a church's daycare.

- In Maryland, a female church music director was awarded $1.35 million after being sexually harassed by the church's pastor.

Twenty years ago, very few people would have considered filing a lawsuit against a church, especially if they were members of the congregation or staff. And in many states, churches used to enjoy immunity from lawsuits under the "charitable immunity" doctrine. Unfortunately, those days are long gone. For whatever reason or combination of reasons, society in general has become increasingly litigious.

Perhaps media coverage of multimillion-dollar lawsuits has contributed to a rise in the greed factor. The recent and highly publicized incidents of alleged sexual abuse by Catholic priests certainly increased the public's awareness of lawsuits against churches. And in many states, trial attorneys frequently run TV commercials promoting their services to people who've been injured or wronged in some way. What's more, it costs a plaintiff little (if any) money to sue a church, because most cases are taken by attorneys on a contingency-fee basis.

We can't pinpoint exactly why litigation has been increasing so dramatically, but we do know this: Over the last decade, there has been a steady rise in the number of lawsuits filed against churches.

Furthermore, while non–church members used to file the majority of cases against churches, the number of congregation members who sue their own churches also has been rising over the past 10 years. Many of these lawsuits stem from issues of negligence, poor supervision of children and youth, unsafe facilities, and improper counseling. Some church staff members have even sued their congregations for wrongful dismissal.

Attacks From All Directions

In today's world, your church can be sued for virtually any reason, even if your organization has done nothing wrong, is not at fault, and has committed no illegal acts. Here are just a few of the actions that can result in a liability lawsuit:

- negligent hiring, supervision, or retention of employees or volunteers;
- sexual misconduct or harassment;
- breach of contract;
- defamation of character, including slander or libel;
- causing emotional distress, either intentionally or through negligence;
- breach of fiduciary responsibility;
- invasion of privacy; and
- wrongful termination of an employee.

Once a lawsuit has been filed against your church, you have no choice but to hire an attorney and defend the church in a court of law. The legal cost of defending against a lawsuit can easily exceed $50,000. Even if you win the lawsuit, you probably will not recover the legal costs.

If your church loses the case, awards for actual damages can easily reach $100,000, and $1 million awards have become increasingly common. Punitive damages could be even higher and can be awarded if an intentional act caused an injury or extreme carelessness contributed to it.

What's more, you can't assume that your church insurance will cover all of the costs. All policies have liability limits and certain exclusions. So your church insurance may cover only a portion of legal costs and damages that are incurred.

Reducing the Threat to the Flock

Church leaders simply have to face the fact that the threat of a lawsuit is greater today than ever before. Therefore, it is absolutely essential to reduce your church's exposure to legal liability. A risk management program can help you accomplish this goal.

For example, even though it's horrifying to imagine, what if a child were sexually abused while he or she was in the care of your church? There is a good chance that the parents of the child would file a lawsuit against your organization on the basis of negligent hiring or negligent supervision. (*Negligence* can be defined as conduct that creates an unreasonable risk of foreseeable harm to others.)

The verdict in this type of case will usually be determined by your answers to the following questions: Did your church have policies and procedures in place for the proper selection and supervision of church employees and volunteers? And if so, how closely were those policies and procedures followed prior to the alleged incident of sexual abuse?

If your church had a risk management program in place that required background checks for all staff members who work with children and outlined specific guidelines for supervision such as the "two unrelated adults" rule, and if these procedures had been followed, your church would be far less likely to be held liable for negligence in the case. In essence, your church would have done everything it could to establish a program that meets the test of reasonable care. And an incident of alleged child sexual abuse is just one of the many possible scenarios that could expose your church to a liability lawsuit.

The point is, if you have a risk management program in place that addresses these types of concerns with established policies and procedures for safety and security, you may prevent the problem from occurring in the first place. At the very least, if the unthinkable does happen and your church is sued, it will demonstrate to a court of law that the church had taken all of the necessary precautions.

More Reasons to Act Now

The possibility of a multimillion-dollar lawsuit is really just one of the many reasons every church should have some type of risk management program in place. If you need additional reasons to convince other leaders in your church that a safety and security program is essential, here are more:

1. Protect your sheep. Above all else, one of the best rationales for a risk management program is to enhance the safety and security of your congregation members—especially those who are the most vulnerable, including children, senior citizens, and disabled individuals. Every person of faith who enters your church deserves to be protected from unnecessary harm.

2. Churches are changing. You and your church are part of an exciting trend taking place across America. Now more than ever, churches like yours are creating innovative ministries, programs, and services to reach out to congregations and communities in amazing new ways. Through your efforts, you are sharing God's love and touching more lives than ever before.

Skateboard ramps and climbing walls are appearing on church campuses. Christian rock concerts take place at some church facilities. Day-care centers are found on many church premises. Programs for seniors have become more common. Homeless shelters, counseling for substance abuse, and international missions are just a few of the new ministries that are being launched each year.

While we all applaud the efforts of today's churches to expand their ministries and explore new ways to spread the Word of God, your organization also must recognize that additional activities and programs expose the church to even greater risks.

3. Bad things can happen everywhere. Don't make the mistake of thinking, "Something like that could never happen here." No matter how safe your church and community may seem to be, bad things can and do happen in churches throughout the country.

Whether your church is located in a quiet little town, affluent suburb, midsized city, or in the heart of a major metropolitan area, no church is immune from crimes, injuries, or accidents. Many of the worst tragedies occur in churches where you would least expect a problem.

4. Churches are targets for crime. Because of the caring and trusting nature of churches, certain criminals actually target houses of worship for unthinkable acts. For example, sexual predators have been known to attend churches just so they can gain quick and easy access to children. And burglars find churches attractive because they know cash and expensive equipment will be stored in the facility, often with little security.

We hope your church has never yet experienced a terrible accident, crime, injury, or other serious problem. But please don't wait until a nightmare occurs to see the need for risk management. If you're proactive and start a program now, you can prevent a host of tragic events. As the old adage goes, an ounce of prevention is worth a pound of cure.

Good Stewardship

Finally, church leaders are responsible for being good caretakers and stewards of the people, property, and gifts entrusted to the church. In short, church leaders have to watch over the flock. Without a risk management program in place, the entire organization is more vulnerable to accidents, injuries, crimes, and lawsuits. But by developing proper risk management procedures, both the leaders and the church itself will benefit from effective stewardship.

The Good News

Although many churches might believe they don't have enough time, resources, or expertise to start a risk management program, those assumptions are not true.

A basic risk management program can be developed relatively easily, quickly, and inexpensively by utilizing the time and talents of volunteers from your church, along with existing information and tools. Even the smallest of churches with virtually no budget is capable of developing basic yet effective risk management programs.

We will show you how to get started by explaining how to

- form a Church Safety and Security Team consisting of qualified volunteers from your church.
- use the EFFECT™ approach to identify and address your church's greatest risks. EFFECT stands for the following:

> Emergency Preparedness
> Facility Safety and Security
> Financial Safeguards
> Employee and Volunteer Safety
> Child and Youth Protection
> Transportation Safety

In general, your Church Safety and Security Team will prioritize its efforts by selecting the most important area in the EFFECT approach, focusing on it first, and then moving on to the next area of greatest concern. You'll also discover how to integrate risk management into your church's everyday activities so it becomes a key ministry that you can be proud of—a ministry blessed with wise shepherds who are good, protective stewards who take seriously the talent of leadership with which God has entrusted them.

Chapter 2

Team Up for Safety and Security

The Answer to a Common Dilemma

Brian, a church administrator, had just returned from a denominational convention, and a task was weighing heavily on his mind.

As he sat at his desk, Brian looked at the notes he had taken during a seminar on church risk management. Many of the stories and statistics the presenter had shared at the seminar had Brian worried:

"Each year, approximately 260 cases of child sexual abuse are reported by Protestant churches."

"A church was sued for over $7 million after a teenager was killed on a hayrack ride sponsored by the church."

"Twenty-five percent of all church fires are caused by arson."

And the list of potential dangers went on and on. Now Brian was more convinced than ever that his church desperately needed to develop some type of a safety and security program to better protect the congregation and organization. The trouble was, he had so much on his plate right now—fundraising for the building addition, hiring a new music director, organizing a mission trip, and preparing for the annual budget review. He simply didn't have enough time to develop a new program on his own.

But if he could get some help, Brian thought, the church could get a program started. At the seminar, he remembered the presenter recommending the creation of a safety and security team made up of volunteers from the congregation. And there were plenty of qualified members who would be perfect for the job. Brian made a mental note to discuss organizing a team at the next board meeting on Wednesday night.

Forming a Safety and Security Team

Based on your own experience, knowledge, and the information presented in Chapter 1, you know why it's critical for your church to establish a comprehensive risk management program.

With your commitment to enhancing safety and security, this can be a great moment in your church's future because you are ready to take one of the most important steps: forming a Church Safety and Security Team. Naturally, you may choose to call this group a different name such as a Church Risk Management Team or the Shepherds Team. But for the sake of discussion, we'll refer to the group as the Church Safety and Security Team, or for brevity, the CSS Team.

While the individuals who serve on your CSS Team will have a number of important responsibilities, they can take great pride knowing they are doing God's work and fulfilling a biblical responsibility to be good shepherds of the flock. They will also be devoting their time and talents to establishing a vital new ministry. Ultimately, the efforts of this team can save lives, protect innocent children, prevent accidents and lawsuits, and strengthen your ministry in exciting new ways. It's a team that can truly make a difference.

Addressing Risks in a Rural Setting

Vinton Baptist Church—Vinton, Ohio

Vinton Baptist Church is surrounded by farm fields and a few small residences. Even though the nearest town is many miles away, Vinton Baptist is thriving because of its ministry to the community. Many of its 350 members are professionals from the region, including teachers, government workers, and local business owners. The church takes pride in reaching out to serve families who are less fortunate and individuals in need.

Because of its quiet, rural setting, there might seem to be little reason for safety or security concerns at Vinton Baptist, but the church recognized that this is not true.

"Unfortunately, drugs and alcohol have become significant problems in the area," Sarah Thornton, director of Christian education at Vinton Baptist, said. "So our church now offers a recovery program on Tuesday nights, which about 90 people attend each week. And we also have recovering individuals who come to our Sunday services."

As Thornton went on to explain, partly because of the church's recovery program, youth ministries, and an on-site day-care center, the church's staff began investigating ways to enhance safety and security.

"After we attended several training courses, heard the statistics, and learned that sexual predators sometimes seek out churches—which is a very scary thought—we decided to establish a Safety Team," Thornton explained.

Vinton Baptist's Safety Team is made up of a lieutenant on the local police force, several state troopers, and other members of the church. For each service and other church events, the Safety Team schedules two members to be on duty.

"The team members dress casually but wear Safety Team badges around their necks so everybody can recognize them," Thornton said. "As part of their responsibilities, they check all of the rooms, walk through the parking lots, visit the playground, and make sure all of the doors and windows are locked at the appropriate times. They fill out a logbook of their activities and also look for anything that could be a potential problem, such as overloaded electrical outlets and other hazards."

In addition to organizing the Safety Team, Vinton Baptist has implemented a variety of other risk management programs. For example, a child abuse prevention policy was developed, and all teachers must complete a training course and give written permission to have their backgrounds and references checked. Red Cross training and workshops on safety are also offered at the church.

"Once we explained why we needed to take these steps, our people were very understanding and receptive to the ideas," Thornton added. "We just want to strive to address concerns as they arise and implement policies and procedures before they become an issue at the church."

How to Begin

Regardless of the size of your church, its ministries, or leadership structure, there are a number of basic principles that apply to virtually every church when forming a team. For instance, one or more advocates of the CSS Team will need to promote the concept and convince church leaders that forming a team is absolutely essential. Qualified members of the team will need to be recruited and selected. The team will require some resources to operate. And the team must meet on a regular basis; gain knowledge; and begin developing programs, policies, and procedures.

In the sections that follow, some general guidelines are provided to help your church establish a strong, knowledgeable, and effective Church Safety and Security Team. Obviously, you will want to tailor and adjust the suggested steps to your church's specific needs, because nobody knows your organization better than you.

Once you've read this chapter, you should start the process and form a team as soon as possible. By putting the team in place, you'll get the ball rolling and establish a foundation to continually enhance safety and security in the years ahead.

Why the CSS Team Is Needed

If a safety or security problem arises at a church, such as a recent burglary, some churches form small ad hoc committees to address the problem. While this is certainly better than not taking action, such ad hoc committees tend to create short-term solutions. If the committee is focused on a single issue, it is difficult to address many other related concerns.

A far more effective, proactive, and long-term solution to safety and security can be achieved by forming a centralized CSS Team to look at the bigger picture, analyze many of the issues facing the church, and develop comprehensive safety and security programs. By forming a CSS Team to coordinate a comprehensive approach, the chances of creating and maintaining a truly safe and secure environment increase dramatically.

In short, a CSS Team is needed to facilitate and oversee all risk management efforts, develop proper policies and procedures, and make sure they are implemented by the church's staff, volunteers, and congregation.

Gain Support From Church Leaders

In order for your church to form a CSS Team and ensure its success, the team will need the approval, endorsement, and support of your church's leadership group, such as the board of directors, clergy members, trustees, elders, deacons, or other administrative bodies. So make sure you and/or another staff member presents the concept of forming a CSS Team. Explain the team's purpose, stress its importance, and gain the group's approval to move forward. In many cases, it takes one or two key people in a church to champion this cause and convince fellow leaders that a CSS Team is absolutely essential.

As with any major initiative, project, or program that your church may launch, it is always best to keep everyone informed and maintain open lines of communication about the CSS Team. Otherwise, if the team is formed without one or more leaders knowing about it, someone may feel left out of the loop. As a result, they may view the effort in a negative light or question its actions. That's why it's so important to get everyone's buy-in right from the start. With universal support and understanding of the team's purpose, the group will have the power to become a valuable asset to the church.

It's also worthy to note that even though the CSS Team should have the blessing and support of the church's pastors or ministers, they do not have to serve as active members on the team. If pastors or ministers want to participate and have the time to spare, they are welcome additions to the team. Often, however, they have far too many other duties and ministries for them to add yet another important responsibility. If this is the case, simply keep the pastors or ministers well informed and allow them to provide input whenever it's appropriate.

In addition, once the CSS Team is in place, it will need to be given the authority to review church activities, develop policies and procedures, and implement them as needed.

Reasons Churches Have Taken Action

Fortunately, there are thousands of churches across America that have already established CSS Teams along with comprehensive risk management programs. At a recent seminar, three different churches with CSS Teams were asked why they felt it was critical to have them and to be working proactively on safety and security concerns. Here are the churches' responses:

Church 1: "We felt it was a matter of being accountable to God for the people and resources under our care. We hold ourselves accountable for how we lead the congregation, and that's what motivated us to act."

Church 2: "At our church, the concept of servant leadership as stated in the Bible is one of our core values: 'Just as the Son of Man did not come to be served, but to serve, and to give his life as a ransom for many' (Matthew 20:28). We believe that taking steps to protect the congregation is consistent with our model of servant leadership."

Church 3: "You can work 80 hours a week year after year to build the ministry up, but all it takes is one incident over the course of a minute or less, and the impact can jeopardize everything that you've work so hard to achieve. Preventing those types of damaging incidents is what our safety and security programs are all about."

Expect Some Resistance

> "The world hates change, yet it is the only thing that has brought progress."
> —CHARLES F. KETTERING
>
> "Change does not change tradition. It strengthens it. Change is a challenge and an opportunity, not a threat."
> —PRINCE PHILIP OF ENGLAND

At nearly every church, there are bound to be certain individuals who are resistant to change. And for whatever reason, there's a good chance you may encounter a few people who do not think a CSS Team is necessary.

At some churches, opponents might feel that a safety and security team could inhibit ministry, stifle creativity, or limit the activities of a particular group. Others may believe the team could encroach upon their territory or area of authority. Or it could be a simple case of naysaying, negativity, or skeptics who feel the team is not needed because the church has been problem-free in the past.

If opposition occurs, be prepared to address it with a spirit of humility and love. Be diplomatic and tactful, but try not to allow a few detractors to stop or postpone the formation of your team indefinitely. The effort is simply too important to be put on hold. So do everything you can to overcome obstacles. Often, even the greatest skeptics will eventually see the value of a CSS Team.

Share the Facts

When facing opposition to forming a Church Safety and Security Team, you may find it helpful to respond with stories and statistics about what could happen if the church does not take this important step. The following are a few facts you can share:

In any given year,
- one in four churches will experience property damage caused by the weather;
- one in five churches will terminate an employee;
- one in seven churches will experience an injury to a child, member, or guest that requires medical care;
- one in eight churches will experience a theft; and
- one in 100 churches will experience an allegation of sexual misconduct.

Minimal Startup Costs

Inform your church leaders that the team will require some initial funding to pay for startup costs, such as the following:

- $100 for educational materials (Many free or very affordable tools, forms, and reference materials are also available online.)
- $100 for subscriptions to church safety resources
- $100 for hands-on training (first aid, CPR, and so on)
- $100 to attend one or more seminars
- $50 for printing and photocopying
- $50 for miscellaneous administrative costs

At many churches, approximately $500 to $1,000 is sufficient to establish a team. This amount can be less or more, depending on the church's budget. If no funds are available at this time, do not let a lack of money stop you. Begin forming your team, and establish a fundraising effort to support the team in the months ahead.

At some point in the future, the CSS Team will probably need to make recommendations that require additional resources from the church. For instance, the team may recommend purchasing a security system. But all recommendations should be submitted to church leadership for approval.

CSS Team Building

With the support of your church's leaders, it's time to begin recruiting volunteers to serve on the CSS Team. Ideally, your team will include between three and eight members, depending on the size of your organization. If your church is large, subcommittees can be assigned in the future as needed. For example, the church may need a separate transportation safety subcommittee to oversee vehicle safety. Initially, however, try to keep the team at a manageable number of members so it can operate efficiently and effectively.

If your church is like many others, it probably has a significant number of members who are well suited to serve on the CSS Team. As a general rule of thumb, try to recruit individuals who have a passion for the church and who represent key ministries that will be affected (such as child and youth programs), and if possible, find people with some type of current or previous experience that applies to safety or security.

Here are several examples of the types of professional backgrounds that are desirable for the team:

- facility or property management
- personnel/human resources
- insurance or safety
- building or construction
- accounting or finance
- law enforcement or military
- fire protection
- legal

In the event that you can't find volunteers with backgrounds similar to those listed above, simply select the best, most qualified volunteers to join the team. Risk management is not rocket science, and most people with skills in project management or problem solving and a dedication to the church can learn whatever they need to know to do an excellent job.

The Recruiting Process

Your church can handle the recruiting process in several ways, depending on what you believe will work best with your congregation.

There's a good chance you may already know individuals who would be perfect for the team. Talk with them personally and encourage them to join. Likewise, you can make an announcement to the congregation that volunteers are needed for the team, or you can place a "help wanted" ad in the church bulletin, newsletter, or on the church's website. You can also send out e-mails and post fliers throughout the church. See the sample recruiting ad or flier below.

JOIN THE CHURCH SAFETY AND SECURITY TEAM

Volunteers Are Needed

If you want to be part of an exciting new ministry that helps protect the people, property, and gifts God has entrusted to our church, consider applying for a position on the new Church Safety and Security Team.

Beginning [date], the team will starting meeting to develop programs to safeguard our church and congregation against property damage, personal injuries, burglary, arson, child sexual abuse, and a host of other dangers.

Serving on the Safety and Security Team is a great way to get involved, demonstrate your commitment to the church, and fulfill the biblical mandate to be a good shepherd of the flock.

For more details and an application, please contact:

[INSERT CONTACT INFORMATION]

_____

[Name]

_____

[Title]

_____

[Phone/E-mail address]

Ask candidates to submit applications prior to a predetermined deadline, and then select the most qualified members. Again, proceed with the recruiting process in whatever manner you feel will be the most effective at your church in the shortest amount of time.

The Long-Lasting Team

We've all seen committees get off to a good start and then fizzle over time. Do not let this happen with your CSS Team. It should become a permanent organization and ministry within your church. When recruiting team members, ask them to make a long-term commitment to the team, such as one year or more. They can accomplish a great deal during the first year of operation, but the team's efforts must be ongoing.

To help ensure the longevity of your CSS Team, consider rotating in new members and leaders as needed so the team remains active, motivated, and productive.

In terms of the team's structure, it's often wise to name or elect a chairperson and co-chair. Among his or her duties, the chairperson can take charge of running the meetings, assigning duties to members, and providing progress reports to the church's leadership group. The co-chair can perform these duties if the chairperson is absent. In addition, the chairperson and co-chair can serve as the primary contacts for the team when someone in the church needs to communicate with the team.

There are, however, no hard-and-fast rules about the structure of your team. It's entirely up to you and your church's discretion to decide the best way to organize the team.

The Order of Business

Initially, it's ideal if your CSS Team can meet on a fairly frequent basis. Then it can move to a less intensive schedule. For example, during the first month, the team can meet once a week and then schedule monthly meetings, ensuring the team gets together as often as necessary to make consistent progress.

The first goal or objective of your CSS Team should be to educate itself on key elements of church risk management. Begin this process by gathering and sharing information, resources, and training materials on risk management topics and procedures. All team members should review the information, become informed, and get up to speed as quickly as possible.

This book is designed to serve as a primary resource for your team. To supplement the information presented here, your team can access other resources as well. Here are some examples:

- The SafeChurch website at www.safechurch.com—As the most comprehensive and interactive site for risk management information, it offers a wide array of resources, features, and tools. Along with the *SafeChurch Resource Packet,* which contains all of the forms, surveys, and other documents referenced in this book, you'll find an automated church risk assessment tool, online video training, project planning capabilities, and so much more.

• The GuideOne Center for Risk Management website at www
.guideone.com—The center provides another extensive collection
of safety and security resources, including checklists, fact sheets,
surveys, articles, and other training materials.

As part of the education process, members of the team should strongly consider
taking appropriate training courses, such as CPR, emergency first aid, and driver
safety instruction. The CSS Team can schedule this training so church staff and
congregation members can participate as well.

Primary Goals

With some dedicated reading and training, your team can quickly gain a basic
understanding of key risk management concepts. While this can usually be
accomplished within a few weeks, the education and training process should
continue in the months ahead so the group can gain additional knowledge and
expertise.

The following are general, recommended goals for a newly formed CSS Team:

1. Become informed about church risk management (safety and security)
   principles, policies, and procedures. Gather risk management information
   and resources, and develop a reference library. Also participate in training
   as needed.
2. Begin to identify your church's greatest areas of risk using the EFFECT
   approach (described in detail in Chapter 3).
3. Determine which single area of risk poses the greatest threat to your church
   and ministries. This top area of risk will become the team's first priority.
4. Develop a plan of action to address the top risk.
5. Create written policies, procedures, and recommendations to minimize the
   risk. Present these to your church's leadership group, and gain approval to
   implement.
6. Roll out new policies and procedures to minimize risks.

One by one, continue to address additional areas of risk and phase in policies
and procedures. Through this approach, your team will develop a comprehensive
risk management program to safeguard your people and property.

Communicate and Involve the Entire Congregation

Once the CSS Team has been formed, it should be introduced to the congregation.
One of the easiest ways to do this is by calling the team together and recognizing
the group during one or more services. Other communications can be used as well,

such as church bulletins, newsletters, and the church's website. Show a photo of the team, if possible, and list everyone's name.

The CSS Team can then begin communicating with the congregation. Messages from the team might include safety reminders, program updates, and invitations to participate in various training courses. An example is shown below. Through these communications, the team can offer helpful reminders and become more visible to all members of the church.

After-Hours Safety Reminder

If you are using the church after regular hours, the Church Safety and Security (CSS) Team wants to remind you to please take all necessary precautions. If you are entering or exiting the church property after dark, please do so in a group of two or more. Be cautious when stepping from a lit to an unlit area. Observe the area around you. And always lock the facility when you leave. We all need to do our part to make our church a safe place to worship. Please watch for more safety and security reminders from your CSS Team.

Also keep in mind that the risk management efforts of the CSS Team will work only if the church's staff, volunteers, and entire congregation understand and support the efforts. Therefore, it's critical for the team to keep everyone involved, gain approval from church leaders on programs and policies, and solicit suggestions from the congregation. The more everyone participates in the new safety and security measures, the more successful the ministry will be in safeguarding your flock.

Chapter 3

Identify Your Church's Greatest Risks

Wilshire Baptist Church is located in an urban area of Dallas, Texas, and has about 3,500 members. When Paul Johnson first joined the organization in 2004 as minister of business administration, he recognized the church was facing a variety of risks that were not being fully addressed.

"Even though the church had taken several key steps in terms of safety and security, it did not have a centralized risk management team in place," Johnson explained. "What we had were a number of programs that had been developed by individual ministries. For instance, the children's and youth ministries had created child safety policies, which were great. But what the church really needed was a more comprehensive approach to risk management."

During Johnson's first year at the church, as part of a due diligence process, he reviewed the safety and security programs the church already had in place. "Essentially, I wanted to identify what we had and what we needed," Johnson explained. "Since the list of needs was fairly long, it was apparent that the best way to get more things done was to go to our governing body and ask them to establish a centralized risk management team."

Johnson's request was approved, and six individuals were recruited to serve on the risk management team, including a property manager, an insurance professional, an attorney, and three other volunteers from the congregation. Johnson provided the team with guidance and a variety of reference materials to get started. "Basically, I asked the team to review the church's current policies and procedures so we could determine what else was needed," Johnson noted. "Then as a group, we sat down and went through a priority process and asked ourselves what things were absolutely the most critical to get done right away. From there, we decided which areas of risk were the highest priorities to tackle first."

Johnson says the team identified three strategic areas where they would concentrate their initial efforts on: finance, a safety egress (evacuation) plan, and first-aid training.

"At the top of our to-do list was to develop financial policies and procedures in a written format. So we asked the church's finance committee to take on that task, which they agreed to do. At the same time, we made arrangements for the church to authorize and conduct its first ever outside audit. As a result of those efforts, we made some major strides in strengthening our financial risk management during the very first year."

The other task that Johnson and the risk management team took on immediately was developing a safety egress plan. (Wilshire's safety egress/evacuation plan is described in Chapter 4.)

Following the initial efforts of the risk management team, Wilshire has gone on to make many other improvements in safety and security. It has developed a comprehensive risk management manual for the church, purchased automated external defibrillators (AEDs), and trained staff members to use the devices. Plus, a wide variety of other new policies and procedures have been created for many areas of the church.

As Johnson likes to point out, the risk management team is now viewed as a permanent committee within the church, but its goal is not to develop programs on its own or to dictate policies. Rather, the team works with various ministries within the church to facilitate program and policy development. Once developed, those programs and policies are reviewed and monitored by the risk management team.

"I think it's absolutely critical for the success of risk management to work with the people who will be affected by the policies and procedures that are being put in place," he concluded. "Safety and security programs always work best if everybody feels they are involved in creating them, have input, and are part of the process."

Time to Roll Up Your Sleeves

We hope that at this point your church has formed or is in the process of forming a Church Safety and Security (CSS) Team. If your CSS Team is already organized and the members are preparing to meet, then you are to be congratulated for taking this essential step. You and the team are ready to roll up your sleeves and get started.

In the weeks and months ahead, each member of the CSS Team will be making an invaluable contribution to the church and its future. By developing programs and policies that safeguard the congregation, the team will be creating a ministry of safety that can be woven into the fabric, philosophy, and culture of the church. For anyone who is motivated by a spirit of concern, compassion, and protection of others, serving on this team will be extremely rewarding.

At one of your first CSS Team meetings, be sure to share your goals with the group (see below):

Overall Goals for the Church Safety and Security Team

1. Become informed about church risk management (safety and security) principles, policies, and procedures. Gather risk management information and resources, and develop a reference library. Also participate in training as needed.
2. Begin to identify your church's greatest areas of risk using the EFFECT approach.
3. Determine which single category of risks poses the greatest threat to your church and ministries. This top area of risk will become the team's first priority.
4. Develop a plan of action to address the top risk category.
5. Create written policies, procedures, and recommendations to minimize the risks. Present these to your church's leadership group, and gain approval to implement.
6. Roll out the new policies and procedures to minimize risks.
7. One by one, continue to address additional areas of risk and phase in policies and procedures. Through the EFFECT approach, your team will develop a comprehensive risk management program to safeguard your people and property.

Off to a Fast Start

As mentioned in goal number one, the first order of business for the CSS Team is to make sure that every team member gains a basic understanding of church risk management and its importance.

One quick way to start the educational process is to have the CSS Team chairperson (or co-chair) gather some general risk management information to share with team members at the first or second meeting. For example, you can ask everyone to read Chapter 1 of this book before your next meeting.

While additional reading, training, and information gathering should continue in the months ahead as your team acquires knowledge and builds a resource library, reviewing the Chapter 1 sections will provide team members with a general overview of risk management and the understanding they need to get started on the next important task: identifying your church's greatest risks.

Breathing a Sigh of Relief

Saturday morning, when John Evans, a church board member, heard motors running outside, he glanced out the office window and saw three vans pulling into the church parking lot. The youth group, which included his son, was just returning from an overnight retreat, and Evans breathed a sigh of relief.

Although he knew the teenagers had been well supervised during the retreat by the youth pastor, an assistant, and three adult chaperones, Evans' biggest worry was the group's safety when they were traveling on the road.

Not long before, the National Highway Traffic Safety Administration (NHTSA) had issued several warnings about 15-passenger vans—just like the ones the church owned and used frequently. The NHTSA studies had shown the vans have an increased risk of rollover accidents under certain conditions. The rollover risks rise dramatically as the number of passengers increase, and improperly inflated tires can add to the danger.

After the NHTSA warnings, the church's new Safety and Security Team, on which Evans served, made van safety its top priority and moved quickly to develop a transportation safety program for the church. It now included driver training, pre- and post-trip inspections of the vans, and a regular maintenance schedule. A fundraising effort was also launched to purchase a new and much safer school bus.

Evans could hardly wait until the new school bus arrived and the vans were replaced. But until then, at least he knew the church was taking extra steps to keep its young people and other passengers safe whenever they were traveling. He walked outside to greet his son and to help perform the post-trip inspection.

Every Church and Ministry Is Unique

Of course, no two churches or ministries are exactly alike. And the types of risks your CSS Team will identify and address depend on the types of ministries and programs your church offers, the size of your facility, its age, location, number of members, the kinds of vehicles it uses, and other factors. Therefore, it will be the team's responsibility to look at your church as a whole, identify which risks are of the greatest concern, prioritize them, and then decide where to focus the CSS Team's immediate attention.

Clearly, identifying and prioritizing risks can be somewhat challenging at first, so to get started, take a look at "The Top 10 Causes of Damages and Injuries at Churches" list on page 36.

As you can see in the list, there are certain risks that are difficult for your church to minimize. For instance, there's not much a church can do to prevent wind and hail damage other than to make sure that roofs and facilities are well maintained. But did you realize that slips and falls are the leading cause of injuries at churches? They can also result in liability lawsuits. Slip and fall injuries are the type of risk that your CSS Team can begin to address immediately.

Also, keep in mind that the list does not include every type of risk. The list is presented here merely to provide your CSS Team with a number of key examples. Depending on your organization's specific needs, you may have different or many additional concerns as well. For instance, while certain risks did not make the "Top 10 List," employment lawsuits, 15-passenger van accidents, and claims against church board members are also significant concerns that churches should consider.

The EFFECT Approach

Your CSS Team can now begin to identify your church's greatest risks by using the EFFECT approach. The EFFECT approach to risk management was first mentioned in Chapter 1, and to serve as a quick reminder, EFFECT stands for **E**mergency Preparedness, **F**acility Safety and Security, **F**inancial Safeguards, **E**mployee and Volunteer Safety, **C**hild and Youth Protection, and **T**ransportation Safety. (See the "EFFECTive Planning" box below for a detailed breakdown of risks for which churches must be accountable.)

EFFECTive Planning

Emergency Preparedness focuses on steps to prepare for emergencies and crises, such as

- natural disasters and pandemics
- fires
- serious illness/injury/death
  - medical emergency during services
  - member/staff emergency during off-site activity
  - key leader's illness, disability, or death
- moral or criminal failure
  - sexual misconduct
  - child molestation at congregational activity
  - criminal involvement by staff or key leader
- terrorism/acts of violence
  - robbery, assault
  - rape
  - shootings or even murder

Facility Safety and Security focuses on steps to address

- facility inspections
- fire prevention
- protecting against slip and fall injuries
- buildings and grounds issues
- hiring of contractors
- use of the church facilities by outside groups
- kitchen/food safety

Financial Safeguards focus on steps to prevent

- theft of church funds
- mishandling/loss of funds
- embezzlement

Employee and Volunteer Safety focuses on steps to address

- worker safety/workers' compensation
- volunteer safety
- employment practices liability
- adult sexual misconduct and counseling
- board member liability
- the expanded role of ushers to enhance safety and security

Child and Youth Protection focuses on steps to enhance

- child abuse prevention
- worker/volunteer selection
- supervision
- responses to allegations of abuse and other misconduct
- nursery safety
- recreational safety, including playgrounds
- Internet safety for young people using church computers

Transportation Safety focuses on steps to address

- owned vehicles—selection and maintenance
- rented vehicles and private vehicles of church members used for church activities
- drivers—selection and training
- occupant safety

Why Use the EFFECT Approach?

Although many churches fully recognize the need to start a safety and security program, it is often difficult to know where to begin and how to proceed with the seemingly complex challenge of developing a comprehensive risk management program.

After working with hundreds of churches across the country on safety and security programs, the Risk Management Team at GuideOne Insurance developed the EFFECT approach. There are three fundamental reasons the EFFECT approach has become popular and successful among churches.

First, the areas within the EFFECT approach are based on extensive research of church insurance claims. The areas help identify the most severe and frequent types of losses that churches experience.

Second, by helping CSS Teams target one area of risk at a time, the EFFECT approach simplifies the process of creating a comprehensive risk management program. By breaking the process into manageable segments, the CSS Team can maintain its focus. And after one area has been addressed, the team can move on to the next area as it expands its scope and adds additional layers of safety and security.

Finally, EFFECT was created to be an easy and memorable way to approach safety and security. It's a concept that everyone can understand and apply within a church setting.

Distribute Two Documents

At one of your CSS Team meetings, provide members with the following documents:

- "The Top 10 Causes of Damages and Injuries at Churches" (p. 36).
- The "Church Risk Identification Worksheet" (p. 37). This document includes seven risk categories team members will be asked to complete.

Ask for Your Team's Input

Show the CSS Team "The Top 10 Causes of Damages and Injuries at Churches" so they can see examples of the most common risks. Then, using the "Church Risk Identification Worksheet," ask everyone in the group to begin naming all of the risks they can think of within each category. Have someone in the group write down all of the risks that are identified by the group and then type them up into a master list. Distribute this master list to the team.

As your team will see, many of the risks that are identified can be placed in one of the six primary categories. Often, risks within each category are directly or indirectly related to each other and can be addressed with similar types of programs and policies. The team may also identify a number of miscellaneous risks as well. These can be addressed at a later time.

Once the team has identified every risk it can think of in each category, review the list and discuss which risks the team believes pose the greatest and most immediate dangers to your church. To do this, it may be helpful to rate each risk on a scale of 1 to 5, with 1 being the most severe type of risk, and 5 being the least severe type of risk.

With So Many Risks, Where Should You Start?

After your CSS Team has completed the "Church Risk Identification Worksheet" and has discussed which risks pose the greatest threats, the next goal will be to decide which area (or category of risks) the team should focus on first.

As the worksheet illustrates, there are a multitude of different risks facing your church that are worthy of your attention. However, it would be extremely difficult or overwhelming to try to tackle everything at once. That's why the best way for many churches to start a risk management program is by selecting one key EFFECT category and focusing the bulk of the team's time and attention on it. Once that area has been addressed, your CSS Team can move on to the next category of greatest concern.

When determining which category to focus on first, it is entirely up to the judgment of your CSS Team—you can begin wherever you like. (It is not necessary to work through the EFFECT categories in order, but each area should be addressed at some point in the future.) Here are some things to consider when selecting your first category:

- If the team has identified several high-priority risks within a particular category, you can start your efforts there.
- If you've identified a risk that's a current "hot topic" among members of your church (such as protecting children from sexual misconduct), it may serve as a good starting point.
- Your CSS Team can take a pragmatic approach. Determine which category can be addressed quickly and economically. Begin with this category.
- If your church has experienced a recent problem or "close call" within a particular category of risks, you may want to focus on this area first.

You're Ready for Program Development

You can have your team members vote on the first risk category or simply reach a general consensus and make a selection. Write your first risk category below, and inform your church's leadership group that this is the area the CSS Team will focus on initially.

The first risk category we will address is:

_____.

Now that you've made your selection, your team is ready to start developing safety and security programs. Next, turn to the appropriate chapter in this book and begin reading. Ask members of the team to read that chapter and gather additional information as needed. (You'll also find a wealth of forms, checklists, and other documents to assist you in the *SafeChurch Resource Packet,* which can be downloaded free from www.safechurch.com.)

Finally, once your team has addressed its first category of risks with the EFFECT approach, remember to revisit the "Church Risk Identification Worksheet" (which you completed earlier) and choose your second category of risks.

> "There are risks and costs to a program of action. But they are far less than the long-range risks and costs of comfortable inaction."
> —JOHN F. KENNEDY

> "A journey of a thousand miles must begin with a single step."
> —CHINESE PROVERB

> "Honors and rewards fall to those who show their good qualities in action."
> —ARISTOTLE

> "Above all, try something."
> —FRANKLIN DELANO ROOSEVELT

The Top 10 Causes of Damages and Injuries at Churches

To help you identify your church's greatest risks, it can be very helpful to know what kinds of risks are the most common among other churches.

GuideOne Insurance, one of the nation's largest church insurance companies, keeps detailed records about the types of insurance claims and losses that churches report across the United States. Based on an analysis of GuideOne's records over the past several years, the company compiled the following list of the most frequent causes of damages and injuries at churches:

- Wind and hail
- Slip and fall injuries
- Water damage
- Theft/burglary/vandalism
- Accidental fires
- Lightning damage
- Recreational activity injuries
- Arson
- Sexual misconduct incidents
- Maintenance injuries

Church Risk Identification Worksheet

One of the most effective ways to develop a church risk management program is by using the EFFECT approach. EFFECT stands for Emergency Preparedness, Facility Safety and Security, Financial Safeguards, Employee and Volunteer Safety, Child and Youth Protection, and Transportation Safety. By identifying risks in each of the categories, you'll be better able to focus your efforts.

Identify your church's risks in the categories below:

Emergency and Crisis Situations (e.g., fire, tornado, heart attack, other medical emergencies, a fatality on-site, criminal investigation)

_____

_____

Facility Risks (e.g., slip and fall injuries, accidental fires, flooding, lightning, burglary, arson, vandalism, wind, storms)

_____

_____

Financial Risks (e.g., theft of church funds, embezzlement)

_____

_____

Employee and Volunteer Risks (e.g., hazardous situations for church employees, volunteers, and other workers)

_____

_____

Child and Youth Risks (e.g., sexual abuse, bodily injuries, accidents during recreational activities)

_____

_____

Transportation Risks (e.g., accidents and injuries when transporting members in church-owned or private vehicles)

_____

_____

Miscellaneous Risks (e.g., injuries at church camp or on mission trips, construction project risks)

_____

_____

Chapter 4

Prepare for Emergencies

Five People Dead After Church Shooting: According to reports by the Associated Press and other news agencies in 2006, a man carrying a gun opened fire at a church service in Baton Rouge, Louisiana. The gunman shot five people—four fatally—and then abducted his estranged wife and her three children.

A few hours later, the gunman was apprehended at an apartment complex near the church after a 911 call. His wife was found dead at the scene from a gunshot wound, but the three children were unharmed. The man was charged with murder, attempted murder, and kidnapping.

The motive for the shooting was unclear, but relatives said the couple had domestic problems in the past. Previously, the wife had filed for a temporary restraining order against her husband, but then lifted it about a month later.

The wife's mother, who also served as church pastor, was wounded in the shooting and left in serious condition. Victims who were killed included the wife's grandparents, a great aunt, and a cousin.

The horrifying incident took place at a small house of worship. Witnesses said the shooter entered the church and started firing his weapon shortly before services were scheduled to end at 10 a.m.

When Tragedy Strikes

While the tragedy that unfolded in Baton Rouge was an isolated incident, it illustrates the type of terrifying emergency that a church can face in today's world.

Unfortunately, the number of crimes committed in and against churches appears to be on the rise.

When it comes to an emergency or crisis situation, a church shooting is obviously a worst-case scenario. Nevertheless, the Baton Rouge incident is a real-life, cautionary example of why churches need to be prepared.

Chances are—and we pray to God—that your church will never experience an emergency like the one in Baton Rouge. But there are many far more common emergencies that occur in churches every day across America.

How Would Your Church Respond?

- During a crowded worship service, a woman collapses in the audience and goes into convulsions.
- A fire breaks out in the church kitchen.
- A tornado or severe storm warning is issued during a large church event.
- A man, apparently intoxicated, enters the sanctuary during a sermon and becomes disruptive.

There may be a number of people at your church who could remain calm, levelheaded, and know exactly how to respond to these types of situations. However, it is more common that employees, volunteers, and members will panic and make the wrong move. A poor decision or improper action during an emergency or crisis can make a bad situation even worse.

Fortunately, if the proper planning, policies, training, and equipment are used, your church can prepare to handle a wide variety of emergencies and crises in the most effective manner possible. Doing so could help prevent a tragedy, keep a situation from escalating, or at least minimize the impact of an unfortunate event.

By reading this chapter and following the suggested steps, procedures, surveys, and forms, your Church Safety and Security (CSS) Team can develop a comprehensive emergency response plan.

Three Steps

Before moving on, let's highlight the three general steps to creating an emergency response plan.

1. **Identify the possible scenarios** (emergencies and crises) that could occur at your church or during a church event.
2. **Use resources** from this book and/or other sources to develop a written

emergency response plan that addresses each of the scenarios identified.

3. **Determine which persons will be responsible for what actions** during the emergency or crisis and how you plan to communicate their responsibilities to them.

In addition, keep in mind that it is extremely important to practice portions of your emergency response plan on a regular basis. A fire drill during a church service is one prime example. Also, review the emergency response plan at least once a year, and make refinements and updates as needed.

Identify Potential Emergencies and Crises

The "Emergency and Crisis Situations" list (p. 56) is a great resource to share with your CSS Team. Likewise, ask members of the group if they can think of any additional scenarios that your congregation could face. Make any additions or deletions to the list that you feel are appropriate, and then prioritize the situations from the most likely to occur to the least likely. In the months ahead, you can develop plans for each situation that you identify. But if you're starting a plan from scratch, it may be helpful to begin with the top three or four scenarios that have the greatest potential to occur.

As you can imagine, each emergency or crisis situation will require a different type of response depending on the circumstances. However, many emergencies and crises can be addressed with similar plans, preparations, and actions. For instance, evacuation plans are essential for fires, gas leaks, and other emergencies. Immediate access to telephones to call 911 and first-aid training are critical for all types of medical emergencies and injuries. And if your church experiences any type of crisis that attracts media attention, it's imperative to have a designated representative for the church who can deliver a thoughtful and consistent message.

Take the Survey

To illustrate a number of the key considerations and actions necessary to develop an emergency response plan, please ask your church's leaders and CSS Team to complete the "Emergency and Crisis Survey for Churches," available in the *SafeChurch Resource Packet* (which can be downloaded at www.safechurch.com).

If your church is anything like thousands of others across the country, you probably had to answer "no" to quite a few of the survey questions. If that is the case, the survey will help you identify many of the elements needed to prepare for an emergency or crisis. It is crucial to address each issue within the survey as you develop a comprehensive emergency response plan.

Plan Development Made Easier

When it comes to the first question in the survey, "Have we created a written and formalized emergency response plan?" we have some very good news. This book and its companion resources will make it a whole lot easier to develop and document your initial plan.

Your emergency response plan should address the following situations:

- fire
- evacuation plan and shelter procedures
- severe weather/natural disaster
- accidents and medical emergencies
- first-aid reminders
- theft and vandalism
- intruders/trespassing/weapons threat
- missing child/persons
- response to an allegation of sexual misconduct against a child
- bomb threat
- gas leaks
- power outage/blackout

In the following pages, we will highlight some of the key steps and considerations for effective emergency and crisis preparation.

An Unexpected Safety Challenge

Wilshire Baptist Church—Dallas, Texas

In Chapter 3, Paul Johnson, minister of business administration at Wilshire Baptist Church in Dallas, Texas, described how his church had formed a safety and security team and had begun to address a variety of risk management issues. To continue Wilshire's story, Johnson and his team encountered an unexpected challenge for their 3,500-member church.

"One of the things we needed to do was establish an evacuation plan and safety egress drill for the entire church facility," Johnson said. "You might think it would be a fairly straightforward process, but it turned out to be more challenging than we imagined."

Wilshire Baptist has built a number of additions to the church over the years, one of which is a three-story building. "We knew we needed a better plan to evacuate that building—especially when it came to elderly people in wheelchairs," Johnson noted. "But when we contacted the local fire department and several other organizations for recommendations, we couldn't seem to get any help. So we had to explore other options and resources to develop our plan."

Johnson said he and his team eventually received assistance and advice from qualified members in the church and several outside sources. "What we finally determined was the need to create 'safe rooms' in the upper levels of the three-story building," Johnson stated. The safe rooms use a "protect in place" strategy for seniors in wheelchairs or others who can't walk out quickly on their own. Safe rooms offer protection until the fire department can arrive and get everybody out. (Note: Once the decision has been made to use a "protect in place" strategy, you must have your plan reviewed by the local authority having jurisdiction over your evacuation plan.)

Thanks to the perseverance of Johnson and the safety and security team, Wilshire Baptist now has an effective evacuation plan for all of its buildings. Safety signage has been installed throughout the facility, and the church is practicing fire drills on a regular basis.

Keys to Effective Emergency and Crisis Planning

Virtually all plans should include these four key elements:

1. **Evacuation Procedures**—Even though the vast majority of churches in America meet local fire codes and have marked exits, it's surprising how many churches have not determined and documented the best routes and procedures for evacuating their buildings. In the event of a fire, gas leak, or other on-site emergency, nothing is more important than getting everyone out of the building quickly and safely. People must also be accounted for once they're outside.

   Evacuation procedures are especially critical for churches that offer Sunday school classes, day care, and nurseries. Elderly members and people with special needs also have to be taken into careful consideration. For instance, if infants need to be evacuated, does the nursery staff know exactly what procedures to follow? Are baby cribs equipped with rollers so they can be easily pushed from the building? Are the doors to the nursery wide enough to accommodate the cribs? Or, if there are a number of elderly individuals who have wheelchairs, how quickly could they be assisted from the building?

   Also, since many churches have constructed multiple additions over the years, the church should evaluate and plan evacuation routes and procedures from those locations as well.

2. **Safe Shelter Inside the Building**—In the event of a tornado, hurricane, or other severe storm, it's critical to identify the safest locations inside the building to seek shelter. A basement is often one of the most secure shelter areas, but if no basement is available, the shelter area should be free of windows. Restrooms and interior hallways on the lowest or ground floor (with doors secured at either end) are other options.

Once shelter areas have been identified at the church, inform staff and congregation members about the locations, and mark the areas with permanent signage on the walls or doors. Storm season is a great time for the CSS Team to publish reminders about the shelter areas in the church bulletin, a newsletter, or via the church website.

3. **Crisis Communication**—Prior to an emergency or disaster, it is vital to determine how your church will communicate with three key audiences: congregation members, the media, and official investigators.

   Congregation Communication—Determine how you will alert the congregation during an emergency. Nearly everyone will recognize the sound of a fire alarm, but consider using a PA system or other method to let people know what is going on and what they should do. Following an emergency or disaster, if the church sustained significant damage, how would you tell members about a temporary meeting place? Techniques for communicating with congregation members include a church website, an e-mail blast, a recorded phone message, text messaging, a phone tree, blogs, and announcements in the local newspaper.

   Media and Investigator Communication—When an emergency, crisis, or tragedy strikes, there's a good chance the church will need to speak with the local media and investigators. Therefore, the church should have a pre-appointed and qualified representative to field all questions. This person should be articulate and have previous experience with media relations and talking with investigators. Without a single representative, the church could make conflicting or inappropriate statements, which may exacerbate the situation or tarnish the church's reputation. The church may also want to appoint a backup representative and consider advising the rest of the staff and leadership to not speak with the media. Instead, refer the media to the pre-appointed and qualified representative.

4. **Disaster Recovery Plan**—What if your church were completely destroyed by a fire, tornado, hurricane, earthquake, or flood? Would it need to shut down indefinitely? Or could it begin operating quickly at another location? Would church leaders have access to important records for financial matters and insurance coverage to rebuild the facility? With a disaster recovery plan in place, your church will have the best chance of surviving a catastrophic event.

   In addition to the crisis communication described in point 3 above, elements of a disaster recovery plan include all of the following, and copies of each of these should be stored in a secure, off-site location:

• a list of important phone numbers, accounts, and addresses
• an itemized inventory of all items, equipment, and other valuables within the church (Photographs and video recordings of items within the church's interior are recommended as well.)
• backup files of computer data and important records
• copies of vital paper records
• the emergency response/disaster recovery plan

Another important step in disaster recovery is to make arrangements ahead of time for an alternative meeting space and equipment. One effective way to do this is to establish a reciprocal agreement with another church allowing use of its facility in the event of a disaster, and its use of yours.

Highlights of Emergency Planning for Common Risks

Depending on where your church is located in the United States, its size, and its ministries, the types of potential emergencies you could face are likely to be somewhat different than other churches. There are, however, a number of common emergency scenarios that most churches should prepare for. In the upcoming sections of this chapter, we will highlight emergency planning procedures that apply to the greatest number of churches. We will cover natural disasters, fire response, terrorism, acts of violence, medical emergency response, leader's death or disability, moral or criminal failure of a staff member, serving as an emergency shelter, and sending out relief workers.

To keep this book a reasonable length, we will not try to include procedures for every type of emergency imaginable. For that reason, we encourage you to supplement this information with additional research and the resources noted in each section. Also keep in mind that various emergencies can be handled with similar plans and approaches. So once you develop a plan for one type of emergency, you'll be able to apply many of the same principles to other scenarios.

Natural Disasters

When the term *natural disaster* is mentioned, one of the first things that comes to mind is the devastation caused by Hurricane Katrina in 2005. With the cost of damages estimated at $35 billion or more, it was the most expensive natural disaster in the country's history, and many churches were destroyed or severely damaged.

Hurricanes are, of course, just one type of natural disaster that may or may not be a concern for your church. Therefore, to keep the discussion general and pertinent to most churches, we will define natural disasters as any of the following: hurricanes, earthquakes, tornadoes, floods, severe storms, lightning, and hail.

Each type of natural disaster requires emergency planning procedures specific to the risks involved, but most procedures fall into these five primary categories:

1. **Building Preparation**—Inspect your facility to determine how safe and secure it will be in the event of a disaster, and make modifications if needed. For example, any trees and limbs that could fall on the building in high winds (or an earthquake) should be removed. Keep roofs well maintained and clean out gutters, eaves, and downspouts. Correct any potential fire hazards, and consider installing lightning rods and electric surge protection. In areas prone to earthquakes, hazards that might fall and cause injuries during a quake should be secured. These include lighting fixtures, pictures, mirrors, and bookshelves. Likewise, adhere to local seismic building standards.

   In addition, make sure appropriate individuals know the location of all utility shut-off switches and valves in case they need to be turned off. Shut-off locations should be documented in the plan.

2. **Safe Shelter Areas in the Building**—As mentioned earlier in this chapter, determine which areas in the building will be the safest places to take shelter during a storm or earthquake. For instance, a basement may provide the best shelter during a tornado, and an interior hallway may be best for an earthquake. Install "safe shelter" signs that describe what type of emergency the area is for, and post maps and directions to the shelter areas throughout the facility. Inform church staff and congregation members about the shelter locations.

3. **Emergency Communication and Training**—Determine how you will alert all church staff and congregation members that they need to take shelter from a storm or earthquake. Staff members and volunteers should also be trained on what to do in the event of an emergency.

   Monitor weather and news reports. Although an earthquake can happen without warning, news reports can provide advance warning of tornadoes and other severe storms. Make sure someone at the church is assigned to monitor weather reports if conditions are threatening.

4. **Store Disaster Supplies**—Keep on hand disaster supplies such as flashlights and extra batteries, portable radios and extra batteries, first-aid kits, emergency food and water, can openers, blankets, soap, toilet paper, and other essential items. Also consider a portable electric generator and spare cell phones.

To enable a church to respond after a disaster, it's wise to keep materials on hand that can be used to make temporary repairs to the church. Doing so can help prevent more costly damage. Examples of useful materials and items include tarps, rolls of plastic, ropes, plywood, tools, wet and dry vacuums, and large fans.

5. **Crisis Communication and Disaster Recovery Procedures**—Preparing for a natural disaster should also include crisis communication and disaster recovery plans. (Please refer to pages 44-45 for details.)

Disaster Resources

For more information about emergency planning for natural disasters, you can check out these resources:

- www.safechurch.com
- www.guideone.com
- www.fema.gov
- www.redcross.org
- www.ready.gov

Fire Response Planning

A fire is one of every church's greatest fears. Not only is it painful to imagine a fire damaging or destroying a beloved building, but worries about injuries and loss of life are the ultimate concern. In the next chapter (Chapter 5, "Facility Safety and Security"), we will take a closer look at risk management procedures to guard against accidental fires and arson. But perhaps even more important is determining how your organization will respond and evacuate the premises during a fire emergency. Elements of a fire response plan should include the following steps:

- Implement facility safeguards to prevent fires (discussed in the next chapter).
- Develop an evacuation plan. This should include carefully designed evacuation routes for all areas of the building. Fire evacuation diagrams should be posted in prominent locations throughout the building.

Evacuation diagrams should clearly illustrate evacuation routes, fire exits, fire alarm pull stations, fire extinguishers, elevators, smoke barriers (fire doors, for example), detection devices (heat, smoke, or flame detectors and local or central station alarm systems), type of construction, sprinkler system, emergency lighting, and heating system.

Put the plan into action. If smoke, a burning odor, or actual flames are detected, take the following steps immediately:

- Pull the closest fire alarm to initiate building evacuation.
- Call 911 and report the location of the fire (address of building), the suspected cause, current status of the fire, and your name and phone number.
- Do not use elevators.
- Exit the building using the closest possible evacuation route.
- After all individuals have exited, close all doors to the immediate area of the fire to help isolate the smoke and flames.
- Follow instructions from the fire department and police.
- Assemble outside the facility at designated areas.
- Account for all individuals once they have assembled in designated areas.
- Go back into the building only after the all-clear signal is given by the fire department.

Practice, practice, practice. To ensure the effectiveness of your evacuation plan, conduct fire drills on a regular basis. At some point during each year, a pre-announced fire drill during a service is recommended so a large number of members are able to take part. Fire drills are the best way to identify weaknesses in the plan and to look for ways to make improvements. Drills also provide staff and volunteers an opportunity to practice their roles and responsibilities.

Terrorism

After September 11, 2001, there was tremendous concern across America about continued terrorist attacks. Fortunately for churches, terrorism focused on religious institutions has not increased dramatically.

Although the threat of terrorism appears to be rather low for churches, it still remains a concern. To help minimize risks, churches are advised to adequately prepare for a single, isolated incident such as the following:

- a menacing person on the premises
- a visitor with a gun
- a hostage or kidnapping event
- harassing or threatening phone calls

• a bomb threat
• a suspicious package

In the next section, we will discuss how to prepare for acts of violence. Many of the steps are equally appropriate for terrorism response.

Acts of Violence

The church shooting in Baton Rouge described at the beginning of this chapter is a terrifying example of the violence that seems to be occurring more frequently in today's society. No one will ever know if that incident could have been prevented with any type of action. But if someone would have noticed the shooter and called police earlier, could one or more lives have been saved?

Many people are surprised to learn that shootings are the most common violent acts committed in churches and schools. Other typical incidents include robberies, assaults, and rapes. As places of trust and compassion, most churches never expect to experience such horrendous crimes. So it's easy to be caught off guard.

In the next section, we offer several suggestions to help your church become better prepared for any potential act of violence.

Make Your Church Less Vulnerable

Designate a Church Security Director—Working with your church's Safety and Security Team, designate a church security director to serve as the point person on security issues. When creating this position, define and communicate the responsibilities of the church security director. In general, the director will help develop, oversee, and implement your security plan.

Develop a Security Plan—This plan should describe guidelines, procedures, and defined roles for all staff persons, including greeters, ushers, and other front-line workers and volunteers. For instance, establish seating and standing locations for all ushers or security personnel so they are strategically positioned in both the front and the rear of the sanctuary. The plan should also include elements such as lockdown procedures for areas of the church; communications techniques; an evacuation plan for the building; and a no-tolerance policy for fights, altercations, and other disruptions.

Facilitate Communications—Establish a method for quickly communicating issues of concern (such as a weapon threat or menacing person) to appropriate church personnel, including the security director and authorities. Depending on the size of your church, walkie-talkies, two-way radios, pagers, and cell phones may be appropriate for effective communications.

Train Your Team—Contact and seek assistance from your local law enforcement agency to provide training for church staff, front-line workers, and volunteers on topics such as violence identification and security methods. Violence intervention training may be appropriate as well. A key goal is to learn how to defuse problems before they become incidents. Also, encourage all team members to openly discuss issues of concern and keep everyone informed about potential situations. (Please refer to the *SafeChurch Resource Packet,* which is free for download from www.safechurch.com, for more details on preparing for and responding to acts of violence.)

Responding to a Violent Incident

If you see a violent act occurring or believe one is about to take place, the first priority is to protect the people in your congregation. To do this, follow these steps:

- Call 911.
- If there is an opportunity to keep the invader out by locking doors and/or closing off areas of the church, do so.
- If there is an opportunity to remove all members and guests from the premises, do so as quickly as possible.
- Quickly control panic. By doing so, you will be more likely to conduct a sequenced evacuation, if possible.
- A leader, such as the pastor or security director, must take charge and provide orders to be followed.
- All orders must be clear and direct, such as the following:
    - "Ushers, secure the building."
    - "[Fill in name], contact the police."
    - "[Fill in name], secure the nursery."
    - "Everyone, take cover on the floor."

Medical Emergency Response

A medical emergency is something nearly every church has experienced or will sometime. Because the likelihood of a medical emergency is so high, a plan for dealing with one should be another key aspect of your emergency response plan. Consider these recommendations as you develop your plan:

- Train ushers and other front-line staff on how to respond to medical emergencies.
- Coordinate and provide first-aid, CPR, and AED (automated external defibrillator) training for ushers, staff, and volunteers.
- Designate a leader to direct others during a medical emergency.
- Identify medical personnel within the congregation, and request their assistance.

In the event of an injury or other medical emergency:
- Call 911 or a designated individual listed on an emergency contact list.
- Identify your location, church name, address, and area of the building to the dispatcher.
- Describe the situation (what happened, type of injury, and help needed).
- Obtain or provide first aid.
- Alert designated church leaders that an emergency is occurring.
- Contact a staff member who has access to any personnel files for medical emergencies.
- Designate an individual to notify the family.
- Station ushers or other volunteers in the parking lot to direct EMTs.
- Practice your medical emergency response procedures.

Prepare for a Leader's Death or Disability

Most churches have one or more leaders who are absolutely vital to the church's success. If such a leader becomes disabled or passes away unexpectedly, his or her absence can leave a tremendous void, disrupt the overall operation, and potentially weaken the ministry. For all of these reasons and more, it's best to prepare for the sadness and impact of a leader's death or disability by taking the following steps:

- Create a succession/continuity plan.
- Secure disability financing/insurance.
- Secure key leader life insurance.
- Designate a media representative.
- Follow the crisis communication plan procedures.

Moral or Criminal Failure of a Staff Member

As disturbing as the thought is, your church must consider the possibility that one of its staff members could commit a sin in the form of an immoral or criminal act. Depending on the type of incident, the church could face a variety of consequences ranging from a lawsuit for negligence to negative publicity. That's why planning for this frightening scenario is critical to maintaining the reputation of the church, mitigating the negative impact, and beginning the healing process more quickly.

We recommend you include the following in this portion of your plan:

- a response policy and procedures for allegations of misconduct,
- a succession/continuity plan,
- a designated media representative, and
- your crisis communication plan procedures.

Serving as an Emergency Shelter

Assisting others in a time of need is part of a religious tradition and why many churches open emergency shelters. If your church wants to take this step, the initial planning of the project is important to ensure a safe operation. As with any project, it is necessary to set goals in line with the resources available. For instance, are there truly enough responsible people who will volunteer to work at the shelter?

Shelter Considerations

Once the decision has been made to offer a shelter, we recommend that you prepare the premises, implement safety procedures, and set rules. Please consider the following:

- Check with local officials concerning the requirements for establishing an emergency shelter. Some localities require shower facilities or other minimum requirements.
- Consult with your local fire department concerning maximum occupancy and fire safety precautions. A good rule of thumb is 45 to 60 square feet of space per occupant and one toilet for every 16 persons.
- Consult with your local law enforcement authorities. They may provide additional security based on the nature of your operation.
- Plan ahead for evacuation of the shelter in the event of a fire or other emergency. Make sure all of your staff and volunteers are made aware of this emergency plan.
- Make sure all exits are clearly marked and have clear access in and out.
- Develop and enforce rules regarding smoking. A prominent display of all rules will help avoid misunderstandings.
- Secure access to other areas of the building.
- Ensure oversight and supervision of the building and occupants. Designate an employee or volunteer from the church as the supervisor of all volunteers. A supervisor should be on-site at all times, and a minimum of two volunteers should be awake at all times to monitor the activity. Staff and volunteers must be trained.
- Don't permit the use or possession of illegal drugs, alcohol, or weapons. Don't allow guests to engage in unlawful or unruly activities. Consider hiring outside security to ensure the safety and security of your guests, volunteers, and building.
- Monitor each entrance and exit to the shelter at all times.
- Clarify with local officials expectations for supplying food, water, and other supplies to individuals housed in the shelter. If the church is expected to provide food and water, make sure that an adequate supply can be obtained and that sufficient personnel will be on hand to distribute these items. Ensure that meals prepared in the church kitchen are prepared only under the supervision of persons trained in

food safety. Follow adequate sanitation procedures concerning food storage, preparation, and serving.

- Follow adequate sanitation procedures concerning bedding, restrooms/showers, and garbage removal. Make sure that you have adequate janitorial support to handle the increased occupancy of your building.
- Plan how the church will respond to persons who contract a communicable disease or who become seriously ill. Contact the local health department for more information.
- Establish set hours so that individuals can't enter after a certain time (for example, no one is allowed to enter the shelter after 10 p.m.).
- Require all guests to complete a guest registration form, and give them a copy of the shelter rules. Require guests to sign in and out daily. Ask each guest to provide you with at least one contact person in case of an emergency.
- Monitor interior and exterior walking surfaces to ensure they're in good condition; adequately lit; and kept free of slip, trip, and fall hazards.
- Don't permit animals or pets, except bona fide service animals for the disabled.
- Eliminate or control hazards that can be expected to attract children (such as discarded large appliances, unprotected equipment, open holes or wells, paths, and stairwells).
- Plan for guests with special needs (such as the elderly and people in wheelchairs and using walkers). Don't allow guests who require medical monitoring.

- Here are some basic rules:
    1. Alcohol or illegal drugs are not permitted on the premises.
    2. Weapons of any kind are not permitted on the premises.
    3. Violence or verbal abuse will not be tolerated.
    4. No one will be admitted after 10 p.m.
    5. A quiet sleeping time will be maintained by 11 p.m.
    6. Smoking is not allowed in the building.
    7. Children should remain with their parent(s) or guardian(s) at all times.
    8. Guests must stay only in the room or area assigned to them and may not wander about in other areas of the facility.
    9. Candles, camping lanterns, oil lamps, and other open flames are prohibited.
    10. Breaking any of the rules will result in guests being asked to leave the shelter.

Proper planning and appropriate safety measures will go a long way toward ensuring that your shelter is a safe operation for everyone involved.

Sending Out Relief Workers

Another act of care and compassion that individuals in your church may feel passionate about is volunteering to serve as relief workers following a disaster. While this is a kind and noble gesture, we highly recommend planning and procedures for relief worker efforts. Consider the following questions and recommendations when providing relief:

- How do we select workers? Establish criteria and qualifications for workers.
- How will we keep them safe? Provide training for workers (Red Cross or denominational).
- What equipment will they be using? Ensure adequate supervision of workers.
- What type of transportation will be needed? Implement transportation safeguards.
- What about liability and insurance? Consult with the church's insurance agent about coverage. Obtain signed release forms from workers.
- Where will they stay?

Final Thoughts

Make your plan accessible. As you develop your emergency response plan, make sure all appropriate church leaders and staff review it and have easy access to the documents. In the event of an emergency or crisis, one or more individuals will need to refer to the plan immediately. Keep several copies of the plan off-site in case the facility is evacuated or destroyed.

What's more, a response plan will not be effective if it's allowed to just sit in a three-ring binder and collect dust. So after your initial plan is created, practice procedures regularly and continue to update and expand the plan as needed.

Use your plan as a training tool. Your emergency response plan can serve as an excellent training tool for staff and volunteers. For example, to train ushers and greeters to respond to medical emergencies, share portions of the plan with them and explain the church's policies and procedures described in the documents. On at least an annual basis, use the plan to conduct an emergency response training course for all appropriate staff and volunteers.

Communicate emergency procedures to the congregation. Don't keep your plan a secret. Let the congregation know that the CSS Team has developed an emergency response plan, and share appropriate information on a periodic basis in church bulletins, e-mails, and fliers posted in the facility.

For instance, if you're located in a part of the country that experiences tornadoes, provide members with tornado safety tips and let them know where to seek shelter in your facility during a tornado warning. Or during colder months when fire risks increase, communicate evacuation procedures so everyone knows how to get out of the building.

Identify medical professionals. As noted in the "Emergency and Crisis Survey for Churches" in the *SafeChurch Resource Packet,* the CSS team should identify all doctors, nurses, and other medical professionals in the congregation and call upon their services if needed. It's also wise to form a Medical Team so arrangements can be made to have one or more team members at every service and key event.

Offer training opportunities. Contact the Red Cross and other organizations and use their expertise to offer first-aid, CPR, AED (automated external defibrillator), and other emergency training courses at your church. Encourage (or require) appropriate staff members and volunteers to participate, and invite the general congregation to take part when class size allows. Anytime your church conducts a recreational event, retreat, or other off-site activity, there should be a minimum of one adult supervisor who has taken first-aid and CPR training.

Keep first-aid kits on hand. Make sure the church has an adequate number of first-aid kits located in key areas of the building. First-aid kits should also be available for off-site activities, retreats, and other events. Check the kits regularly to make sure they're well stocked.

Facilitate immediate communications. All key staff members and volunteers should have immediate access to telephones or other communications devices to call for emergency responders if needed. As cell phones have become commonplace, this precaution is much easier and more affordable today. During every church activity, all appropriate staff—including ushers, greeters, Sunday school teachers, choir directors, activity supervisors, youth pastors, and others—should be equipped with a cell phone or walkie-talkie or have immediate access to a land-line phone.

Now Is the Time to Prepare

In reality, too many churches get caught off guard when facing an emergency or crisis. So please do not wait until an urgent situation strikes your church to recognize the need for planning and preparation. By acting now, taking the necessary steps, and developing an emergency response plan, your church will be better able to handle just about any situation that arises.

Emergency and Crisis Situations

Even though nobody likes to imagine the scary things that can happen, it's important to recognize that urgent situations can and do occur in churches on a frequent basis. The following are examples of emergencies and crises that many churches have faced:

- weather emergencies (tornado, hurricane, flood, lightning, blizzard)
- medical emergencies (heart attack, stroke, seizures)
- fires (accidental and arson)
- injuries (on-site or at an off-site church event)
- armed robberies or burglaries
- vehicle accidents involving church members
- gas leaks
- major equipment breakdowns such as broken water pipes or a cracked boiler
- allegations and investigations of crimes committed by a church employee, volunteer, or congregation member
- local media attention during a crisis or after a tragic event
- bomb threats
- assaults on church members or leaders
- a suspicious or threatening intruder
- kidnapping
- criminal activity on church grounds
- a suicidal member
- terrorism
- harassing or obscene phone calls

Chapter 5

Facility Safety and Security

A 5-Gallon Bucket of Keys

When Brad Janowski joined Calvary Church in Muscatine, Iowa, as the full-time church business administrator, Calvary was preparing to move to a new, much larger facility to accommodate its 1,600 members.

"The church had purchased a vacant shopping center for the new campus, which would quadruple our size in terms of square footage," Janowski said. The new facility is located next to a major four-lane highway in a commercial area of town. A Target store, car dealership, and other large merchants are nearby. "When we were preparing for the move, I recognized that we would need to greatly increase our safety and security efforts at the new campus."

With Janowski's extensive background in facility security administration and his work for the state's department of corrections, he was well aware of the risks the church could face at the new location.

During the period leading up to the move, Janowski began taking a number of important steps, such as forming a new Safety and Security Team. "One of the first things I did was gather a group of people together who I felt would be qualified for the team, including individuals in law enforcement, firefighters, EMTs, and an ex-military man," Janowski explained. "I asked the group to start looking at things we could do to boost the level of safety and security at the new campus. The group came back to me with a number of recommendations for policies and procedures.

Some of them would require time and resources, while others were simple, but still very important."

For example, Janowski and the team felt that far too many people had keys to the old church:

"According to our records, more than 200 keys had been issued to various members over the years. And I don't know how many times I came to work in the morning and found that somebody had forgotten to lock the front door of the church the night before. So at our final service at the old location, I carried a 5-gallon bucket to the front of the sanctuary and asked everyone who had a key to bring it up. When we were done, the bucket was almost full. We probably collected over 300 keys, and I don't think we got all of them."

For the new Calvary campus, a more restrictive policy for key distribution was established. "Now the only people who have keys to the new Calvary campus are church employees," Janowski stated. "We tell everyone at the church, if they need to get in, all they have to do is let us know when and where, and we'll have a staff member let them in. Initially, a few people balked at the rule, but now everyone is used to it, and the church is much more secure."

Since moving to their new campus, Janowski and his team have implemented many other effective policies and procedures to safeguard the church and its members. In upcoming sections and chapters, we'll highlight more of the great things that Calvary Church is doing.

It's a More Dangerous Time

Back in the "good ol' days," many churches could leave their doors unlocked with little if any worry about intruders, theft, vandalism, arson, and other problems. It seemed that even bad guys viewed churches as sacred places that should not be violated.

Unfortunately, those days have long since passed as society has changed, morals have declined, and drug addiction has increased. Today, due in part to the vulnerability of churches, religious institutions are actually targets for criminal acts. For example, the rising price of scrap copper has led thieves to target churches. Entire air-conditioning units have been stolen in increasing numbers from churches for their copper components. During a recent six-month period, losses of over $1 million from church copper thefts were reported to GuideOne Insurance alone.

The potential for a lawsuit against your church is yet another growing danger. While several years ago most people would never have considered suing a church, that is no longer the case. Society has grown increasingly litigious, and the chance that a church will be sued by a guest, member, or individuals working on-site is greater than ever before. In Texas, for example, an elderly woman tripped over a pothole in her church's parking lot and fell, breaking her hip. She later died from complications from the initial injury. The woman's family sued the church and recovered $125,000 for its negligent failure to maintain the parking lot.

Potential crimes and potential lawsuits are just two reasons it's important for your church to focus on facility safety and security. Equally critical are steps to guard against accidental fires, slip and fall injuries, water and storm damage, and many other property losses.

Most Common Church Facility Risks

- wind and hail damage
- slip and fall injuries
- water damage
- structural damage
- crime
- accidental fires
- arson
- lightning and surge losses
- outside contractors
- facility usage by outside groups

It's Easy to Get Started

No church wants to experience the problems, costs, or tragedies that facility risks can cause. Therefore, by reviewing this chapter with your Church Safety and Security (CSS) Team and using the accompanying surveys and checklists in the *SafeChurch Resource Packet* (downloadable at www.safechurch.com), you and your team will be able to do the following:

- identify the most common church property risks and hazards;
- know how to perform regular, detailed inspections;
- recognize risks/hazards when you encounter them during a church inspection; and
- know how to address the risks/hazards by performing maintenance, repairs, and modifications to enhance safety and security.

To help you and your CSS Team get started, please complete the "General Church Property Survey" in the *SafeChurch Resource Packet.* As the survey illustrates, there are many basic steps that your church can take to make its facility safer and more secure. By addressing facility safety and security issues with a proactive, comprehensive plan, you can prevent problems before they occur; avoid interruptions to your ministry; and provide a safer environment for your church members, visitors, and staff.

In the sections that follow, we will walk you through some of the key procedures and most common facility-related concerns, and provide recommendations to address them.

Perform Regular Inspections

Paint cans left near the church's furnace, frayed extension cords, overloaded electrical outlets, a loose handrail in a stairwell, damaged shingles, faulty wiring—if hazards such as these go unnoticed and are left uncorrected, they can lead to significant damage or serious injuries.

Identifying hazards is one of the reasons it's so critical to inspect the building's interior and exterior on a regular and scheduled basis. Ongoing inspections will also help your church identify and remedy situations that can increase the likelihood of break-ins, burglary, arson, and other crimes.

The inspection process should be overseen and/or conducted by members of the CSS Team. You should consider three levels of inspections to optimize safety. First, it's a good idea for ushers or other volunteers to conduct weekly inspections immediately before worship services to identify hazards such as walkway obstructions or burned-out light bulbs that might be a safety risk to persons attending church that day. Any hazards noted should be corrected immediately, or if that's not possible, warnings should be posted and the affected area should be cordoned off until a repair can be made.

Monthly inspections are highly recommended as the second level of inspection. These inspections should be conducted in conjunction with the church's CSS Team or committee responsible for the church property. Finally, a thorough inspection of the property should be completed once each year. As part of its overall inspection process, the team is advised to develop a checklist and document the inspections, needed repairs/modifications, repair dates, service work, and so on.

To assist your team with inspections of the facility, please refer to these three inspection forms in the *SafeChurch Resource Packet* (available at www.safechurch. com): "Monthly Inspection Checklist," "Annual Inspection Checklist," and "Security Checklist."

In addition, the inspection process will be far more effective if it includes professional assistance from certified contractors and local authorities. For instance, heating, ventilation, and air-conditioning systems should be inspected and serviced by a certified contractor each spring and fall. The electrical system should be inspected annually by a certified electrical contractor, particularly if the building is older. And fire extinguishers, sprinkler systems, and fire detection systems should be inspected annually by local authorities and/or certified contractors. Also, ask your insurance company if an on-site risk management (loss control) inspection can be arranged.

During the inspections, your church should be on the lookout for a wide variety of hazards and risks such as uneven walkways and sidewalks, parking lot disrepair, hazards at entrances or in hallways and stairways, and improperly stored combustible materials. Then take appropriate steps to eliminate the hazards and minimize risks. Now let's take a closer look at key considerations for facility safety and security.

Wind and Hail Protection

To a certain extent, your church is at the mercy of high winds and hail. But since these weather conditions are leading causes of damage to churches, a number of important steps should be taken to prevent or minimize damage.

Inspect trees near the facility. Severe storms often blow down tree limbs or entire trees, which fall on buildings and cause severe damage. Therefore, if your church has any trees or limbs that are too close to the facility, they should be trimmed or removed. Large, older trees are a special concern. Although the trees might be beautiful, portions of the tree may be decaying from the inside and could easily break and fall.

Maintain roofs. In the "Prevent Costly Water Damage" section of this chapter, we'll stress the importance of roof maintenance. Maintaining a roof that is in good, sturdy condition is also essential to avoid excess damage in high winds or hail. In hail-prone areas, consider installing impact-resistant shingles with Underwriter Laboratories (UL) designations of 2218, Class 3 or 4.

Identify vulnerabilities to wind. During your monthly inspections of the church, look for things that could be damaged by high winds or items that could be blown in the air and cause damage. For example, is there a gutter, downspout, or awning that needs repair? Or does the church have unsecured signs, lawn furniture, or playground equipment that could become airborne? If so, take steps to repair or secure items.

Inspect windows. If the church has older single-pane windows, consider upgrading to modern double-pane windows with shatter-resistant glass. Also have stained-glass windows inspected to ensure their integrity and strength. Consider protecting them by installing a protective covering on the exterior.

Keep the entire facility well maintained. In general, a well-maintained building will have the best chance of weathering all types of storms with the least amount of damage. Churches in areas with hurricane exposure should follow all normal procedures for storm preparation such as boarding up windows and other precautions.

Prevent Slip and Fall Injuries

One of the easiest and most important steps that your CSS Team can take to enhance facility safety is working to prevent slip and fall injuries. Many churches underestimate how common, severe, and costly these types of accidents can be.

During a recent Christmas season, a congregation member arrived at church for a Tuesday morning Bible study carrying packages of presents in both arms for the other members of the group. Outside, the church's automatic sprinkler system had been left on even though temperatures had recently dropped below freezing. This created ice on the church's sidewalk. The member slipped backward on the ice and struck her head. She never regained consciousness and passed away because of head injuries.

Obviously, a death caused by a slip and fall is the worst possible scenario. But it's important to recognize how frequently people get hurt when they slip and fall. According to GuideOne Insurance company records, slips and falls are the number one cause of injuries at churches as well as liability claims. What's more, churches are frequently sued by people who are injured on the premises. So instead of keeping your fingers crossed in the hope that an injury will not occur, you and your team should be proactive in helping your church prevent slips and falls.

Preventing Slips and Falls

Use church inspections to identify these common slip and fall hazards:
- uneven surfaces
- parking lot disrepair
- unexpected obstacles on walking surfaces
- poor lighting
- hazards at building entrances
- snow, ice, or water on walking surfaces
- loose or missing handrails
- loose carpeting

Monitor these high-risk areas during inspections:
- doorways, door thresholds, and doorstops
- playgrounds
- sidewalks

- stairwells
- places where electrical extension cords and tools are being used
- kitchen areas
- parking lots

Solutions to Prevent Slips and Falls

- Conduct regular inspections of the church premises.
- Make any needed repairs to carpeting, sidewalks, parking lots, handrails, playgrounds, and so on.
- Install additional lighting in dark areas.
- Use yellow, no-slip paint on curbs to alert pedestrians of changes in elevation.
- Install no-slip treads on wooden stairs and interior ramps or inclines.
- Direct runoff water from roofs and downspouts away from walking areas.
- Use "Wet Floor" signs when cleaning and mopping.
- Avoid painting walkways.
- Place protective guardrails around floor openings, lofts, and other open areas.
- Warn of hazards that have not yet been repaired.
- Encourage visitors to slow down and take small steps when surfaces are slick.
- Maintain proper snow and ice removal, use salt and sand applications, and keep records of the actions taken. The records may be necessary to help defend against a liability lawsuit.

Prevent Costly Water Damage

Water damage is the third most common cause of property losses at churches according to insurance claims data. From frozen pipes that break, leaking roofs, and drain blockages to sewer lines that back up and overflow, the damage caused by these types of problems can be extremely costly to repair. They can also disrupt a ministry by preventing use of the building.

The sooner you spot symptoms of water damage, the better the chances are of avoiding a larger, more costly problem. As part of the inspection process, be on the lookout for signs of current or past water damage, including the following:

- rotten wood;
- damaged walls;
- stained ceiling panels and rusty light fixtures;
- dampness or standing water in the basement; and
- leaking faucets, pipes, and toilet fixtures.

If any water damage is discovered, the church should act as quickly as possible to correct the situation and repair the damaged area.

If a storm sewer or sanitary sewer backs up, it can damage the church's foundation, walls, floor coverings, appliances, equipment, and valuables. Raw sewage can also enter the facility, creating a horrible smell and health hazard that is expensive to clean up. It's important to establish basic policies in order to protect your church facility from this threat.

Sewer Backup Prevention

To help prevent a sewer from backing up, take the following precautions:

- Do not pour grease down sinks or toilets.
- Use strainers in sinks to catch food scraps, and dispose of them in garbage cans.
- Instruct visitors not to put solid waste (disposable diapers and personal hygiene products) in the toilets.
- Do not connect floor drains, drain tiles, downspouts, and sump pumps to the sewer line.
- Do not plant deep-rooted landscaping on top of or next to the sewer laterals.
- Install a cleanout.
- Install a sump pump to remove unwanted, excess water.
- Install a backflow-prevention device.
- Recycle yard waste.
- Keep valuable items on shelves, or keep important documents or valuables out of the basement.
- Install flooring that is less susceptible to water damage.
- Make sure all doors to exterior basement stairwells are adequately caulked and weather-stripped.

Keep a Good Roof Over Your Head

One of the key ways to prevent water damage is to make sure the church's roof is in good condition. As roofs age and are exposed to the elements over time, or if they are damaged by a storm, a leak can develop and cause significant damage. So it's important to regularly inspect and monitor the condition of your facility's roof. The individual(s) who inspects the roof should be qualified to do so and understand what to look for in terms of damage and condition. For instance, look for cracking, blistering, cupping, or peeling of asphalt shingles, which affect the roof's ability to divert water from rain, snow, or melting ice. Also, ensure that flashing or coping around the edge of the roof is in good condition. And hire a qualified, licensed roofing contractor to make necessary repairs.

When looking at roof replacement options, consider materials that can help mitigate future damage. As an example, in hail-prone areas, consider impact-resistant shingles with Underwriter Laboratories (UL) designations of 2218, Class 3 or 4. For maintenance, keep gutters, eaves, and downspouts in good condition and free of obstructions, and remove snow from roofs to prevent potential collapse.

On a related note, you should also monitor the condition of the facility's exterior walls. Deteriorated soffits, siding, and trim can allow water to penetrate the structure. Any damaged wall material should be repaired or replaced.

Baptisteries Pose Water Risks

Churches with baptisteries are at additional risk for water damage. Many baptisteries are constructed of fiberglass and hold hundreds of gallons of water, so if the tank is overfilled or develops a leak, severe water damage can result.

As baptisteries are being filled, monitor them carefully to prevent overflow. Also inspect all water lines, the interior of the tank, and connections for leaks. If there is an overflow prevention pipe installed, make sure it is clear.

Keep Pipes From Freezing and Breaking

Just about everyone knows that when water freezes inside a pipe, the water expands, putting pressure on the pipe, which can cause it to break. The result can be costly water damage and substantial plumbing repair bills.

Pipes that are particularly vulnerable to freezing are those located outside and in unheated areas or along exterior walls with little or no insulation. Frozen pipes are also a concern in Southern states if the facility has minimal or no insulation in an attic or crawl space.

Frozen Pipe Prevention

- Remove garden hoses from exterior faucets before winter.
- Shut off and drain water supply to outdoor faucets and sprinkler systems.
- Wrap pipes exposed to freezing temperatures with pipe insulation.
- Seal areas with cold air drafts (crawl spaces, attics, garages, and outside walls).
- In older buildings with poor insulation in exterior walls, open doors of cabinets on exterior walls where pipes are located, and turn faucets on to a slow drip.
- Maintain the heating system properly.
- Consider installing an automatic water-detection system.
- If the church will be unoccupied for an extended period, set the thermostat to at least 50 degrees Fahrenheit and check the building daily.
- In vacant or unheated buildings, shut off the main water valve, drain all lines, and put nontoxic antifreeze in trapped waterlines.

Consider Replacing Galvanized Steel Pipes

Copper and steel are the most common types of pipes used in buildings. But until the 1950s, galvanized steel pipes were widely used for plumbing systems. Since galvanized steel pipes are prone to corrosion, they increase the potential for water damage. Corrosion of galvanized pipes leads to restricted water flow and eventually causes the pipes to leak and fail. If your church was constructed before the 1950s, there's a chance it may have galvanized steel pipes. If so, consider hiring a certified contractor to replace the pipes with copper ones. Copper pipes are more expensive than steel but more durable.

Check for Structural Damage

Along with inspecting for water damage, keep your eyes open for any signs that may indicate structural damage to a building, such as cracks in exterior walls; bulging, bowing, or leaning walls; deteriorated masonry components; and a damaged or sagging roof.

If you discover any problems, hire a structural engineer to determine the extent of the problem. Based on his or her recommendations, hire a professional contractor to make any necessary repairs. Even though structural repairs can be somewhat costly, it's far more affordable to correct the problem now, before it gets worse. Furthermore, in situations with sagging roofs or leaning walls, occupant safety is the primary concern.

For churches that have one or more buildings of masonry construction, deteriorated or cracked mortar joints between brick are of particular concern. Tuck-pointing (repairing mortar joints) should be done as needed by a qualified craftsman. If the building is more than 20 years old, it should be evaluated by a qualified contractor now and at least every 10 years.

Secure Your Facility to Prevent Burglary, Vandalism, and Other Crimes

Each year, thousands of churches are burglarized in the United States, and an increasing number of churches are experiencing vandalism, arson, and other frightening crimes. While it was unimaginable just a few years ago, we must also now worry about the possibility of terrorism.

Theft, burglary, and vandalism—combined—now represent the fourth most common reason for church insurance claims. We may never know exactly why more crimes are being committed against churches today, but one thing is clear: Without sufficient security, your church, members, and possessions are more vulnerable than ever before. If security precautions are not taken, your church is easy prey. (Precautions for crimes against people are addressed more fully in Chapter 4. Precautions against property crimes are addressed here.)

Security-Related Risks

Consider the security risks your church may face:

- burglary and theft of property (One burglary occurs every 14.7 seconds in the United States.)
- robbery (Collections, which frequently include cash, may be targeted.)
- vandalism to the exterior and interior of your facility
- auto break-ins in church parking lots
- arson (According to the U.S. Fire Administration, one out of four church fires is arson-related.)
- shootings or other acts of violence
- child abductions
- terrorism

Basic Precautions: The Five L's

There are five basic precautions that your church can take to enhance the security of your facility and surrounding property. We call these the "Five L's" of crime prevention. We advise you to implement as many of these precautions as possible to reduce the risk of various crimes.

Lock up—Make sure that doors and windows are locked when the building is unoccupied. Use 1-inch deadbolt locks on exterior doors. Doors should be made of solid core (not hollow) construction and, if hinged on the outside, should have tamper-proof hinges. Lock windows with locks positioned so they cannot be opened if an intruder were to break the glass. Likewise, consider burglar-resistant or wire-mesh glass windows.

Also, maintain key control, particularly when there has been a turnover in employees. Lock up ladders, tools, and flammable materials such as cleaning supplies and gasoline at the end of the day. And secure stairways and fire escapes that provide access to the roof. Use only high-quality padlocks on overhead doors, loading docks, and so on.

Lighting—Illuminate building exteriors, doors, and parking lots from sunset to sunrise. Update timers for exterior lights following time changes and consider installing motion-activated lighting near doors and windows.

Landscaping—Keep shrubs and trees trimmed around windows and doors to eliminate potential hiding places for arsonists and criminals. Consider prickly or thorny plants beneath lower-level windows to discourage break-ins. Do not allow signs or displays to block the view of the building. And pick up trash and other combustible materials from church property.

Lookout—Establish a "Church Watch" program in which members volunteer to drive through the property at various times throughout the week and alert police to anything suspicious. Also, ask neighbors to contact police to report suspicious persons or activities.

Law enforcement—Develop positive relationships with local police, and invite them to patrol the property at odd hours. Familiarize police with times of worship and church activities so they'll be alerted when people are unexpectedly present.

For an example of a "Security Checklist" that your church can use or modify, please refer to the sample in the *SafeChurch Resource Packet* (downloadable for free at www.safechurch.com).

Control Access to the Facility

In the introduction to this chapter, which featured Calvary Church, you read about an all-too-common situation in which too many people have keys to the facility. Although the practice makes it convenient for members who need to get inside, keys are easily lost, stolen, and duplicated, and some people may forget to lock doors when leaving. The church should also know who is in the facility at any given time.

In some parts of the country, especially in smaller towns, there are still churches that resist locking their doors because they feel the community is safe or believe a locked door runs counter to a ministry that's warm and welcoming. But like it or not, every church has to recognize that people with bad intentions can show up anywhere, at any time. An unlocked door is an open invitation to theft, vandalism, arson, trespassing, and vagrancy.

To prevent a needless problem, churches are strongly advised to have a policy for controlling access to the building, particularly when it is unattended.

How to Control Access to Your Facility

- Lock all buildings when they are not in use.
- Limit key distribution, and document those who possess a key.
- Consider distributing keys to employees only so they can let members inside.
- Rekey or replace a lock when a key is lost.

- Eliminate or limit the use of a master key.
- Keep any backup keys in a locked box.
- Before locking up the church, perform a walk-through to check for open doors and windows and running faucets and toilets, and to verify that no one else is in the building.

For Greater Protection

To further safeguard your property and people, consider installing a security system. Statistics show that a security system can significantly reduce the chances of a burglary or break-in. Depending on the type of system installed, it can also enhance the safety of your church's staff and congregation.

Security System Safeguards

In general, a system can be designed to provide a number of fundamental safeguards or "lines of defense." The system you choose can provide one, several, or all of the following: intrusion protection/burglar alarm system, off-site 24-hour monitoring service, access control to the facility (for example, the use of electronic door locks on the entrance), video monitoring and/or recording, and additional automation and integration (for example, intrusion protection and smoke/heat detection equipment can be integrated with 24-hour monitoring).

For many churches, installing a burglar alarm, or an "intrusion detection system," should be a high priority. High-quality burglar alarm systems are available from a variety of companies, and again, there are many features, accessories, and technologies to choose from. But no matter how basic or sophisticated an intrusion system may be, it has four primary objectives:

1. **Deter**—Criminology studies indicate that most burglars will avoid buildings with an alarm system. This is one reason security companies usually place decals or signs on windows, doors, and other areas of the property that state "Protected by ABC Security System." If would-be burglars see there is a security system installed, they will often leave the building and look for an easier target.

2. **Detect**—Through the use of various detection components such as glass-break sensors, a security system will detect an attempted or actual break-in.

3. **Alert**—In the event of an attempted break-in or actual entry, most systems will set off a loud, audible alarm. This alerts anyone in the neighborhood that a break-in may have occurred. If the system is monitored by an off-site service, the event will be reported to the appropriate local authorities, who will be dispatched to the scene.

4. Frighten—Finally, the audible alarm will usually frighten intruders, which may keep them from entering the building or get them out quickly if they're already inside.

Intrusion System Options

Here are just a few of the detection devices that can be incorporated into a system:

- glass-break sensors (detect vibration and the sound of falling glass)
- motion detectors (detect a moving person or object in a designated area)
- magnetic door/window contacts (detect entry through doors and windows)
- outdoor sirens and strobes (provide audible and visual alarms outside the building)
- photoelectric beams (detect an intruder in the path of the beam)
- dock plugs (magnetic switches used for protecting movable objects)
- line-cut monitors (sound an alarm if a phone line is cut)

Since most churches have limited budgets, the cost of a security system may seem prohibitive. But with technological advances today, there are many less expensive alternatives. Keep in mind that the risks are real and that the cost of a crime could be high. Much like insurance, a security system can actually save your church money. If your church loses several thousand dollars' worth of equipment in a burglary, your insurance may cover most of the cost. But the church will still have to pay the deductible to replace the equipment, which may be $500 to $1,000 or higher, as well as cope with the inconvenience of damaged or missing equipment until it can be repaired or replaced.

You don't need to turn your church into a fortress or buy the most expensive security system to protect it. A basic, high-quality burglar alarm system can be a very effective deterrent. Systems can also be designed so they are unobtrusive and will not detract from your ministry.

Build Relationships With Police and Firefighters

As Brad Janowski, church business administrator for Calvary Church in Muscatine, Iowa, pointed out, one of the most effective and economical ways to improve church security and safety is to build relationships with local authorities.

"Our church has great relationships with law enforcement people, firefighters, and EMS teams in the community because we've made a conscious effort to reach out to them, support their efforts, and become their friends," Janowski explained.

Janowski said Calvary Church uses a variety of programs that help strengthen relationships. For instance, on an annual basis Calvary hosts a special law enforcement and firefighter appreciation day at the church. "During the service, we honor and thank those individuals for the work they do and the sacrifices they make and for protecting the community," Janowski said.

At Thanksgiving and Christmas, the church takes meals to the local fire stations to feed firefighters and EMS personnel who are on duty during the holidays. Also, on a regular basis, Calvary invites the local fire department to come out and tour the campus so they are familiar with the church's layout and emergency equipment. Cookies, coffee, and doughnuts are provided to the firefighters as a gesture of the church's appreciation.

In addition, twice each year Calvary allows the police department to come out and conduct vehicle training in the church's 6-acre parking lot. The police SWAT team has permission to train in the building. And Janowski welcomes any officer who simply wants to stop by the church and have a cup of coffee.

According to Janowski, having a close working relationship with law enforcement and firefighters really pays off. "One time, I received a call at 3 a.m. from a police officer, who found a door open at the church. So not only was he driving around our campus, he got out to check all of the doors."

During another incident, Janowski and one of his staff members encountered a man at the church who asked for money and became belligerent. "I called 911 and told the dispatcher we needed some help," Janowski recalled. "A few minutes later we had six squad cars pull up. You simply can't buy that kind of protection."

"The way I look at it is, if you work at cultivating the relationships, you'll receive great service and response," Janowski added. "This is something any church can do."

Fire Prevention and Safety

Throughout the United States, a fire occurs in a home or building every 80 seconds, and arson is the leading cause of all commercial building fires.

The thought of a fire is especially terrifying for a church. Loss of a life or serious injuries are the worst tragedies imaginable. Even a small fire can cause smoke and water damage that shuts the church down for weeks. And if the church is severely damaged or completely destroyed, the ministry could be disrupted indefinitely.

Due to the inherent dangers of a fire, it is essential for your church to develop and implement a fire prevention and safety program. While your church may already have a number of fire-related safeguards in place, the real question is this: Are there more steps your church can take to protect its people and property? If your church is like most churches, the answer is "yes."

Three Objectives

A fire prevention and safety program has three fundamental objectives: first, to put preventive measures in place that reduce the risk of fire; second, to protect lives if a fire breaks out; and third, to minimize damage if a fire occurs.

Inspect the Facility

As mentioned earlier in this chapter, a primary responsibility of the CSS Team is to make sure the interior and exterior of the church (and all structures) are inspected on a regular, scheduled basis. For the inspection process, the team should develop a checklist and document actions for fire prevention, safety, and procedures to minimize fire damage. Record details such as fire hazards, needed repairs, dates of inspections, and service work.

Naturally, your church will need to develop a fire prevention and safety program that is customized to meet its specific needs. In general, though, there are four areas that your team should consider: (1) structure, equipment, and maintenance; (2) congregation and staff safety; (3) arson prevention; and (4) future enhancements. (See "Key Areas for Fire Safety Consideration" in the *SafeChurch Resource Packet* [downloadable at www.safechurch.com] for important advice as you implement your fire safety program.)

Initially and periodically, it is wise to get professional assistance for fire-related recommendations during the inspections. The local fire department, state building inspector, electrician, and heating system specialists are excellent resources.

Baptist Church Discovers a Fire Hazard

When a Baptist church in Illinois was being inspected for a new insurance policy, a fire hazard was identified in the church's older electrical system, which utilized fuses instead of modern-day circuit breakers. Before writing the policy, the insurer asked the church to install Fustat devices on the electrical system to reduce the risk of fire. (Fustats are safety adapters that are installed into socket-style fuse holders. The Fustat devices help prevent the use of oversized fuses on electrical circuits, which could overload the system and cause a fire.)

The church agreed to make the modification and replaced 87 Edison-based fuses (most of them 30 amp) with 15 and 20 amp Fustat holders and Fustat fuses. The cost of the materials was only $300, and an electrician was hired to test the load of all circuits and correctly size the Fustat fuses.

As a result of the inspection, discovery of the hazard, and addition of Fustats, the church has greatly improved the safety of the electrical system in its historic facility. There's a good chance it may have also prevented a fire.

The Foundation of a Plan

We hope the information in this chapter has provided you with a good, general overview of some of the key elements and procedures necessary to enhance facility safety and security. There are, of course, other facility-related issues that were not addressed, such as security in child care areas, safety for maintenance workers, and financial safeguards. Those subjects will be covered in upcoming chapters. For details about church kitchen safeguards, see the *SafeChurch Resource Packet* at www.safechurch.com; also see Chapter 10 for important information on facility topics including:

- Allowing Others to Use Your Church
- Hiring Outside Contractors
- Construction Safeguards

Since every church is different, we realize you may have additional facility concerns that are entirely unique to your building, location, or organization. For those, we suggest seeking professional advice and doing further research. In the meantime, this book is designed to provide your CSS Team with the information, resources, and tools to create the foundation for a basic yet effective facility safety and security plan.

Chapter 6

Financial Safeguards

In Indiana, a 70-year-old grandmother and longtime bookkeeper at a Methodist church is awaiting her sentence for embezzling $113,000 from the church over a period of at least five years.

"About six months after I joined the church in 2005, I could see there were very few checks and balances in place when it came to our finances," the Methodist pastor said. "Right after we started working to improve our accounting and reporting practices, the theft was reported."

As the pastor explained, when the church's bookkeeper learned that new accounting procedures were being established, she began to destroy financial records in an effort to hide her actions. Another employee at the church noticed the missing records, became suspicious, and asked the bookkeeper about them.

"The woman knew she was going to be caught, so she came to me and confessed," recalled the pastor. "At that point, we had no choice but to report it to the police, who investigated the incident and turned it over to the prosecutor's office."

To determine how much money had been lost, the church hired an accounting firm to review the financial records. "Even though some records were destroyed, the accountants were able to go back four or five years and determined that at least $113,000 had been taken," the pastor said. "Basically, the bookkeeper was writing her own payroll checks and then reconciling the account. That lack of oversight and structure made the theft possible."

Now an outside firm handles payroll, and the church has established many other financial safeguards. "We're using standard accounting practices now, separation of duties, checks and balances, background checks, and other procedures," the pastor noted. A "rule of two" has also been established that requires two unrelated adults to be present whenever money is being handled.

"We've been discussing the theft and the actions we've taken in hopes that it will help other churches avoid a similar experience," the pastor concluded. "I also think it's important to stress that the real reason for having financial safeguards in a religious setting is to protect people's integrity and their standing with the church."

Church Burglary in Colorado

According to a report in a Colorado newspaper, a church was burglarized in March 2006. The break-in occurred during the early hours of a Monday morning, and the offering money collected from Sunday services was stolen from the church's office. As the pastor stated, the only time the church kept a significant amount of money on the premises was after Sunday services, before the bank opened on Monday and deposits could be made. The amount stolen in the burglary was not disclosed, but it included cash and checks from the church's two locations.

$800,000 Stolen From Oregon Church

In 2007, a woman who served as the longtime comptroller of a Presbyterian church was facing charges of aggravated theft in connection to $800,000 embezzled from the church. The woman accused of the crime was solely responsible for the church's financial bookkeeping for more than 10 years.

Detectives were alerted about suspicions of missing funds when a member of the church's finance committee discovered discrepancies in the accounting records. After hiring an accounting firm to audit the church's records, the firm found that at least $800,000 had been embezzled during the comptroller's career with the church. Police said the woman was apparently writing checks to herself and then altering records to show the money was being spent on church services and various needs. The church put the woman on administrative leave; she later resigned and is awaiting her court date. This incident was reported in a southern Oregon newspaper.

Don't Be in the News

It's always disheartening to hear news reports about a thief stealing money from a church during a burglary or other type of robbery. But when church funds are stolen because of the actions of a trusted member or employee, the crime is even more shocking.

How could a respected individual, who appears to have the highest morals and integrity, commit such a sin? While the motives for most crimes can never be fully understood, temptation, greed, gambling problems, debt, addictions, and mental illness are frequently cited by criminals who have been caught stealing from churches.

Theft, loss, mishandling, and embezzlement of church funds are situations that no church leader wants to consider. The possibility of a crime seems especially out of place in a church setting that fosters compassion and trust. Nevertheless, these crimes do occur far more frequently than you might imagine.

The sad truth is, one in five churches in the United States will experience some type of theft or burglary this year.

The Responsibility of Financial Stewardship

As you know, every church needs resources in order to operate. And with costs continuing to rise, it's imperative to protect each dollar your church receives so every penny can be put to good use. We must also consider the kindness and generosity of the people and groups who provide funding for our churches. They tithe and donate their hard-earned money believing the gifts will be guarded and used prudently to do God's work.

In the spirit of proper stewardship, it's essential for churches to be vigilant and cautious about monetary resources. If adequate safeguards are not put into place, your church could risk losing hundreds, even thousands, of dollars in precious resources.

Your church may already be taking a number of precautions to protect its finances. If so, we salute those efforts. But maybe your church could take additional steps to create even higher levels of protection. Or, if your church is one of the many that have few or no safeguards in place, now is the time to act, before your church makes front-page news.

Aunt Mildred's Purse

To avoid embarrassment, we will not identify the following church and member by their actual names. Yet how many churches do you know that use a similar approach to handling Sunday offerings?

Mildred Mason—68 and affectionately known as Aunt Mildred—has been a member of her small-town church for more than 41 years. She serves on the church's board and is loved and trusted by the entire congregation.

Each Sunday, after the offering trays have been passed, they are placed at the front of the sanctuary near the pastor. When the sermon has concluded and everyone is leaving the sanctuary, it's Aunt Mildred's responsibility to retrieve the offering trays and take them to the church office. There, she counts the cash and checks, puts the money in two envelopes, and prepares a deposit slip for the bank. When her accounting duties are finished, Mildred tucks the envelopes safely into her purse and goes home to prepare dinner. First thing on Monday morning, she takes the church's funds to the bank.

Aunt Mildred has never kept a penny of the church's money for herself, nor would she ever consider it. She even uses her own money to pay for the gas to drive to the bank each Monday. But what if, heaven forbid, Mildred's purse were snatched as she walked to her car, or what if her home were broken into on a Sunday night? By simply possessing the cash and checks, her safety would be at risk. Or what if she accidentally were to lose one of the envelopes? Would her good name, reputation, and standing in the church be called into question?

A Few May Question the Need

When the need for financial safeguards is raised, some people in the church may resist changes or feel they are unnecessary. A common reaction is, "That could never happen here; everyone is totally honest." But the truth is, thefts can and do occur at many churches where crime is least expected.

Another common concern is, "Will it look like we're being too suspicious or paranoid?" The answer to those questions is a resounding "no." The number one goal of financial safeguards is to protect the money and resources that God has given to the church. Equally important, financial safeguards will help protect the reputations of church employees and volunteers who are involved with finances.

Imagine for a moment that one of your members is solely responsible for a cash box during a busy church event. For just one minute, he leaves the box unattended while getting his coat, returns, and finds the box is almost empty. When he reports the theft, could it look like he was at fault or even took the money? You know he would never steal a dime, but could someone else think otherwise?

On a much larger scale, what if hundreds or thousands of dollars in church expenses cannot be accounted for because of a lax check-writing policy? Could one of the church leaders be accused of misappropriating the funds for his or her own use?

Those are just two unfortunate scenarios that financial safeguards could help prevent. In addition to protecting funds, avoiding the appearance of impropriety is another great reason for financial safeguards.

Three Types of Financial Risks

At a high level, there are three types of financial risks that every church should consider and address:

Internal Risks—Embezzlement, misappropriation, mishandling, or loss of funds by church staff or volunteers such as bookkeepers, treasurers, or financial volunteers

External Risks—Thieves, burglars, and other criminals who might steal church funds (This now includes Internet scams and other electronic crimes.)

Tax and Regulatory Risks—Failure to comply with government regulations, improper financial reporting, tax implications of unrelated business income, risks to nonprofit status, and so on

In the sections that follow, the bulk of the information will focus on reducing risks in the first two categories. Because of the complexity of tax and regulatory risks, which vary by church and state, we will not attempt to address them in this book. Instead, we strongly encourage your church to consult with qualified accountants, attorneys, and other professionals to seek advice and develop a plan.

In addition, an important part of protecting your church's finances is making sure your church is adequately insured. This chapter will conclude by addressing several key considerations for insuring your church.

Create a Written Financial Safeguards Plan

Ask your church leaders and Church Safety and Security (CSS) Team to complete the "Financial Safeguards Survey," available in your *SafeChurch Resource Packet* (downloadable at www.safechurch.com). This survey provides a quick and easy way to identify key areas where financial safeguards may be needed at your church.

Once you're read the remaining sections of this chapter, you and your CSS Team will be able to create a written Financial Safeguards Plan that specifies the proper policies and procedures for how money is collected, handled, deposited, reported, and audited.

Written financial policies and procedures let the congregation know that you are committed to financial integrity and are protecting the security of their contributions. Policies and procedures are also essential to communicate the church's expectations and requirements to individuals who handle finances. Additionally, the Financial Safeguards Plan will clearly define the staff's and volunteers' responsibilities and provide an effective deterrent to any wrongdoing. (See "Getting Started on a Plan" on page 80.)

Getting Started on a Plan

Begin by developing a list that describes your current procedures for handling money and finances in all the situations you can identify. Consider the following:

- Collections during Sunday service—How is the money collected? Where is it placed? Who counts it? How is it deposited in the bank?
- Bank accounts—Who oversees the accounts? Who has access to the checking account and is authorized to write checks and make withdrawals? Who reviews the bank statements?
- Bills and invoices—Who receives them? Does anyone double-check them for accuracy? Who is responsible for writing the checks? Does the same person sign the checks?
- Fundraising campaigns—Who receives the checks? How are they handled and recorded? Who makes the deposits?
- Petty cash—Where is it stored? Who has access to it? Who authorizes use? How are records kept?
- Special events—Who collects the funds? Are the amounts recorded? Who deposits the money?
- Bookkeeping and audits—Who keeps the books, and how is accounting for the church handled? Are the financial records audited or reviewed by an outside source on a regular basis?
- Church credit card(s)—Who has access to cards, and how are purchases approved, monitored, and tracked?
- Financial communication—How is the church's financial situation communicated to the congregation?

Once the CSS Team has identified all of the ways the church receives money, handles it, and conducts other financial matters, you can begin to develop proper policies and procedures as part of your overall Financial Safeguards Plan. The plan should address procedures for handling funds from the time collections are taken to until the money is disbursed.

By creating this plan, the church can help prevent the accidental loss of funds or intentional thefts. The risk of embezzlement will be greatly reduced as well because everyone will know that the church's finances are being carefully monitored with checks and balances. This plan will also help protect both staff members and volunteers if an accusation is ever made.

Proper Handling of Collections

Money doesn't sit still at Calvary Church in Muscatine, Iowa. "We have a very large auditorium with lots of activity going on," Brad Janowski, church business administrator at the 1,600-member church, noted. "So we now have a written policy for exactly how we collect the offerings—what we do with the funds, how they're handled, and where they go." As Janowski explained, "Within five minutes of collecting the offering, it goes into a bank bag, and two members of our church security team take the offering and drop it in our bank's night deposit box. That way, it doesn't stay here, on-site. Our service goes on during the deposit process, and the crew is back from the bank before the service ends. We then retrieve the offering at a later time for counting."

Train Ushers as the First Line of Security

At many churches, ushers are used to pass offering plates and gather collections. If your church uses this common practice, it is critical to select ushers carefully, stress the importance of their roles, and train them to perform their duties with care and awareness of potential risks. When ushers know what their responsibilities are and what steps should be taken, they can play a vital role in protecting the church's funds.

As part of an usher's job, he or she should be instructed to watch for anyone who seems out of place in the audience or is behaving suspiciously. If such a person is spotted, one usher should alert a church leader with either verbal or nonverbal communication so the suspicious person can be monitored from a distance. Ushers should also watch the collection plates as they are being passed.

In most instances when there are no concerns, everything goes smoothly, and the collection is complete, two unrelated ushers should take the money and checks to a secure location, where the collection is locked up, preferably in a sturdy safe, so it can be counted later. This practice is much less risky than taking collections to the front of the church or another area and leaving the funds unattended. If a thief happened to be present, he or she could easily see where the funds were sitting.

Adhere to the "Two Unrelated Adults" Rule

Two unrelated adults should always monitor the handling of church funds. This "two unrelated adults" rule should apply from the time money is collected and secured to when it is deposited in the bank.

Even though a husband-and-wife team or other related individuals can be extremely trustworthy, it is much better if the people handling the money have no direct relationship with each other. This is another way to avoid the possible appearance of impropriety. If any funds disappeared accidentally or intentionally, an unrelated person would be more likely to report it.

Use Teams to Count Funds

Once collections have been received and are placed in a secure location, some churches choose to count the money immediately after services have concluded, while other churches prefer to count the next day. If your church is going to count the next day, make sure funds are stored in a heavy-duty safe (if possible, in a double-locked room).

Regardless of when the collection is counted, a team of individuals in a locked room should perform the task. All envelopes, cash, checks, and coins should remain visible to everyone throughout the counting process. The team should double-check, confirm, and balance the amounts. Then the team should complete a form that lists the amount of all currency and checks, sign the form, and keep it on file. Finally, a deposit slip for the bank should be filled out.

It's highly recommended to rotate members of the counting team on a weekly or monthly basis. And above all else, never allow collections to be taken home for counting or deposit. Doing so only puts the individual's safety and reputation at risk if something bad were to happen.

Additional Safeguards for Offerings

- Encourage members to write checks instead of giving cash.
- Checks received in collections should immediately be stamped with a restrictive endorsement such as "For deposit only."
- Use an envelope system to deter theft of loose cash or coins from the offering.

Be Careful When Making Deposits

Two unrelated adults should be placed in charge of making bank deposits for the church. Before these adults transport the funds, all currency, checks, and coins should be placed in a bank bag and then concealed in another nondescript bag to carry outside.

As hard as it may be to imagine, a criminal could actually be watching your church to see if there is a predictable routine when money is carried from the facility. So try to vary the team members and departure times, and alter the routes driven to the bank when making deposits.

Upon arriving at the bank, look around the parking lot to see if there are any suspicious vehicles or individuals waiting around, especially if making a deposit after hours. If everything looks safe, proceed to make the deposit by either using the drop box or entering the bank.

Overseeing the Petty Cash Fund and Pastor's Discretionary Fund

The purpose of a petty cash fund should be to cover small, unanticipated expenses that need to be paid immediately, such as postage due and COD deliveries. Funding for larger expenditures should be planned and handled through the church's regular purchasing process described in the next section of this chapter.

For petty cash funds, establish a small cash limit that is kept in the custody of a designated office worker. Guidelines concerning appropriate uses of the fund should be communicated to all appropriate personnel. The fund should be stored in a locked location, and distributions from the fund should be documented. When the fund balance falls below a predetermined amount, documentation of the expenditures should be submitted before the fund is replenished. The fund should be subject to periodic, unannounced audits.

Many churches have a pastor's discretionary or benevolence fund that is kept separately from the church's main checking account. The purpose of this fund is to address benevolent or other charitable requests that come to the pastor's attention and that, typically, the beneficiary wishes to be kept confidential. While discretion is a legitimate concern, guidelines should be established by the church board to avoid financial irregularities with the discretionary fund and to protect the pastor from unwanted tax implications.

These guidelines should address how money in the fund is to be used, how distributions should be documented, and how often and what amounts may be given. Checks should never be made out to "cash." Bank statements from the fund should be reconciled by a person not involved in check writing, and periodic, unannounced audits of the fund should be performed.

Establish a Purchase System

To ensure accountability, all purchases should be made through a voucher system in which check requests are accompanied by appropriate paperwork supporting the expense. Purchases over a specified amount should require the approval of a church or ministry leader. If anything is purchased with personal funds, a receipt and form for reimbursement should be used.

Guarding Against Embezzlement

According to the FBI, the profile of a typical embezzler is someone who has been on the job for five to six years; delivers above-average performance; and is highly motivated, valued, and trusted. In other words, most embezzlers are the people you would least suspect.

Despite who they appear to be, however, many embezzlers have committed similar crimes in the past. As many as 70 percent of embezzlers are reported to be repeat offenders.

After reviewing hundreds of incidents of church embezzlement and internal theft over the years, GuideOne Insurance has identified two common patterns that have enabled most of the crimes to occur: (1) A longtime employee or volunteer is so well trusted that no one checks or audits his or her work, or (2) a pastor (or other church leader) has so much authority in the church that nobody questions the decisions he or she makes, including those involving church finances.

If your church has a staff member who falls into one of the two categories mentioned above, we certainly do not want to call his or her honesty or morals into question. It's important, however, for you and other church leaders to be aware of the types of situations that lead to most cases of embezzlement, theft, and fraud. Unfortunately, as statistics show, these types of crimes are usually committed by people who have served the church for years, are trusted implicitly, and are respected by all.

Granted, your church may be fortunate enough to have never experienced a case of embezzlement or internal theft. But why place your congregation at risk? There are so many no-cost or low-cost safeguards that can be implemented to greatly reduce the risks. Although the steps may require a small amount of additional work, every honest employee and volunteer should be more than willing to comply. Don't settle for mom-and-pop style accounting practices. Even the smallest churches handle thousands of dollars each year and need to do so responsibly and professionally.

Regardless of the size of your church and whether your budget is large or small, it's simply wise stewardship to put financial safeguards in place. One such safeguard is screening the employees and volunteers who handle finances.

Screen Employees and Volunteers Who Handle Finances

As mentioned in the opening of this section, approximately 70 percent of embezzlers are repeat offenders. This is just one reason it's important to screen the people in your church who play financial roles. Screening should include the following:

- An application process in which the prospective worker completes an application that provides information about previous employment, church involvement, volunteer work, and references.

- Checking references. Be sure to call places where the individual has previously worked or volunteered in a position of trust involving finances.
- A criminal background check.
- A credit check on financial employees such as bookkeepers, financial secretaries, business managers, treasurers, and finance directors.

Obtain Bonding for Financial Workers

To provide the church with added protection from any losses stemming from embezzlement or misappropriation of funds, we highly recommend bonding for employees and volunteers who handle church funds. The topic of bonding can be confusing to the average person, but essentially it involves a special kind of insurance that protects the church against an employee's dishonesty. To obtain bonding, churches should contact their insurance agent to discuss fidelity or dishonesty insurance coverage to protect against dishonest acts by employees.

Develop Internal Controls for Checks and Balances

Internal financial controls is a fancy term for a system of checks and balances to prevent embezzlement and improper use of funds. To a large extent, internal controls create separation of duties between individuals who handle finances, such as the counting team, treasurer, bookkeeper, and church's financial secretary.

If your church is like many others, a few people serve multiple financial roles. While that can seem great from an efficiency standpoint or even necessary due to a limited number of volunteers, overlapping responsibilities can invite abuse. Therefore, we strongly advise separation of duties.

For example, the person who prepares checks for the church should not have the authority to sign the checks. On the other side, the person who has check-signing authority should not have access to blank checks or sign checks made out to "cash." If the amount of a check is over a predetermined amount, it's wise to require two signatures. As another separation of duties, the church's bank statement should be opened and reviewed by someone who is not involved in writing checks.

Key Internal Controls

- Separate duties of those responsible for writing checks, signing checks, reconciling bank statements, and preparing financial reports.
- Establish an authorized process for approval of expenses before issuing payment.

- Develop a voucher system so that all checks are supported by an original invoice and requisition request for payment. Supporting documents should be canceled by stamping "paid" on the paperwork when a check is issued.
- Enforce a policy that no checks are to be made payable to "cash."
- Authorize more than one check signer, but check signers should not be given access to blank checks or sign checks made payable to themselves.
- Require dual signatures for checks over a predetermined amount.
- Keep checking account signatures up to date with your financial institution.
- Be sure that bank statements are opened and reviewed by a person other than the check writer or signer.
- Ensure canceled checks are reviewed by someone who is on the lookout for unusual patterns such as dual endorsements or unfamiliar vendor names.
- Protect accounting records, and keep them in a secured location. Accounting software program data should be backed up regularly as well.
- Schedule an annual audit or financial review of the books by a qualified person not involved in the church's financial operations. (This will be covered in more detail later in this chapter.)

Credit Card Precautions

Church credit cards for authorized users can be convenient financial tools, but precautions are essential to prevent misuse. At one church, for instance, a secretary obtained a church credit card in her name when other cards were being issued for the ministers. The secretary used her credit card for personal expenses, which the church paid for without knowing. Eventually, her secret came to light when a minister's card was declined as he attempted to register for a seminar. Upon investigation, it was learned the secretary had charged nearly $100,000 in personal expenses on the church's account. She was arrested and charged for her criminal acts.

Safeguards Against Credit Card Abuse

- The church's credit card program and credit limits should be reviewed and approved by the board, finance committee, or other governing body.
- Written procedures should be in place for the credit card program, including a description of appropriate and inappropriate expenditures, documentation required for reimbursement, timely submission of card statements and receipts, rules prohibiting personal use and cash advances, and mandating a return of the card upon termination of employment.

- Each user should sign documentation for the credit card, acknowledging receipt of the card, agreement to abide by the credit card policy, acceptance of financial responsibility for personal expenditures, and agreement to return the card if employment ends.
- The church should select a credit card issuer/provider that will allow it to maintain central control of the account, including the authority to do the following:
  - preclude individual users from changing credit limits
  - prohibit transactions involving certain vendors or categories of vendors
  - turn off the cash advance option
  - eliminate offers to users regarding additional cards, balance transfers, and/or increases in credit limits
- Notify the card issuer immediately if the billing statement is incorrect or missing, or if a credit card is lost or stolen.
- Discuss credit card fraud protection with the card issuer.
- Prohibit credit card use by the bookkeeper or other individuals responsible for credit card payments.
- Have the treasurer or other financial officer regularly review credit card statements and payments.
- Periodically run business credit reports.
- Educate users on protecting credit card information.
- Immediately close credit card accounts of employees who terminate employment with the church.

Conduct Financial Audits Regularly

At one church, the bookkeeper pleaded guilty to embezzling $365,000 by writing checks to herself over a period of years. Although the checks were supposed to have had two signatures on them in order to clear at the bank, most of the checks were signed solely by the bookkeeper. Authorities believe that if the church's books had been audited regularly, this case of embezzlement would have been caught in the early stages.

In general, there are three goals for conducting an audit of the church's financial records: first, to promote an environment of accountability; second, to receive a "management letter" from the auditor that indicates any weaknesses in the church's accounting system; and third, to protect the integrity and reputation of church leaders who oversee church finances.

Ideally, the church's financial records should be audited by an outside certified public accountant (CPA). Most audits by CPAs provide church leaders with a "management letter" that identifies areas of weakness in the church's financial operations. The recommendations within the management letter may include serious concerns and corrective actions that should be taken when needed.

While an annual audit by an outside CPA is highly recommended, it may not be feasible each year for some churches due to the expenses involved. Therefore, if a complete CPA audit is not possible every year, churches should use other options to have their books reviewed in the years between formal audits. Additional options include the following:

- CPA review or compilation—a less extensive review and analysis of the church's financial records by an outside accountant provided at a lower cost. This does not provide the level of detail or management recommendations of an audit.
- Internal audit committee—an internal church committee composed of members with finance backgrounds who review the church's financial reports and records for discrepancies or areas of concern. Members should not have been involved with church financial operations during the period of review. This is a no-cost option.
- Review by another church treasurer or accountant—a non-CPA review of the church's records by an outside individual with knowledge of church finances. This has the benefit of an "independent" review without the qualifications or extensive detail of an outside CPA audit. This is the least expensive "outside" option.

Safeguards for External Risks

In Chapter 5 we discussed a number of key ways to protect your building from arson and break-ins. As a quick reminder, the chapter covered the use of security systems/alarms, the "5 L's" of crime prevention, and the importance of establishing close relationships with local law enforcement agencies. Since much of that information applies equally to safeguarding your finances from external risks including burglary and other types of theft, please refer to Chapter 5 for important details.

If security measures are not in place during office hours at your church, it is possible that a suspicious person or vagrant could enter the building and pose a threat. Even if such individuals may not intend to rob the church or commit another crime, it is extremely important for the church staff to have a planned response to help ensure their personal safety.

Office Hours Safeguards

- Control access to the building during weekdays by keeping all exterior doors locked.
- Use an intercom with an electronic door release system to admit persons to the building.
- Maintain a physical barrier in the reception area such as a glass partition, countertop, or half door.
- Have all visitors sign in at a guest registry. You can also issue a visitor's badge in exchange for their identification and/or require that visitors be escorted while on the premises.
- Install a panic button in the office that activates an alert in other areas of the building. Or the button can provide a direct alarm to police.
- Establish a code word or distress signal that will alert co-workers to a problem. For example, if church workers typically address each other by first names, establish a code that if someone is in distress, he or she will address a co-worker more formally and by his or her last name.
- Workers should not be alone in the office. If being alone is unavoidable, all doors should be locked.
- Individuals seeking assistance should be screened by providing identification and completing a request form to verify their need.
- Only non-cash assistance such as food or gas cards, tokens, or vouchers should be supplied.
- Do not maintain large sums of cash in the office.
- Do not confront a suspicious person on church property. Report the individual to police, and observe him or her from a distance.
- Do not hesitate to call 911 if you or a co-worker feels your personal safety is at risk.

Computer and Internet Safeguards

In today's electronic age, churches face a number of relatively new threats that should be considered and addressed in your Financial Safeguards Plan. They include:

- e-mail scams/solicitations in which the sender attempts to trick the recipient into sending money or products—often to a distant country.
- "phishing" scams in which the sender tries to trick the recipient into providing confidential information in order to access bank accounts or credit card accounts and/or to steal the recipient's identity. In many cases, these e-mails include hyperlinks to sites that appear to be legitimate, but aren't.
- computer hackers who may try to gain access to financial records.
- computer viruses that can destroy important financial records.

> • spyware or "Trojan horse" viruses that can be used to steal confidential information.

Electronic thieves are now using a wide variety of scams to target churches. In one case, churches were being asked to contribute to a charitable cause that did not exist. So it's important for everyone at your church who uses a computer with Internet access to be on guard and take the proper precautions. Suggested safeguards for computer use are highlighted in the "Digital Security" box below. If you need further assistance, seek out an information technology (IT) professional from the congregation or hire a local technician.

Digital Security

- Install antivirus software on all computers and keep it up to date.
- Install fire-wall protection.
- Install anti-spam filters and software.
- If youngsters at the church have computer access, install filters and software to block pornographic content.
- Train staff members and volunteers who use computers to be on the lookout for fraudulent e-mails and Internet scams. If an offer sounds too good to be true or someone "in need" is asking for money, it's probably a scam.
- Never provide confidential information, including bank account numbers (church or personal), when requested to do so in an e-mail. If you're uncertain whether the e-mail actually came from a legitimate service provider or vendor, visit the website.
- Never download a file unless you're sure it's from a safe, legitimate source.
- Scan all files for viruses before downloading.
- Use password protection, and change passwords regularly.

Electronic Giving Safeguards

Another trend emerging among churches today is electronic giving. When this book was published, research showed that 12 percent of churches were allowing members to make contributions via electronic funds transfer (EFT). To give electronically, members authorize the church to have a pledge or tithe automatically debited to the members' checking or savings account at a predetermined time each month. While this new form of giving is convenient and efficient, it also creates a number of financial concerns. If your church is considering an electronic giving program or is using one already, please keep these issues in mind:

- Research and select your EFT provider carefully. Banks and EFT processing companies are offering electronic giving services. Before signing up for service with any institution, make sure the program is safe and secure. The institution should have security measures in place to prevent fraud and unauthorized use.
- Seek indemnity from the EFT provider. An important protection to request is a clause in which the provider agrees to indemnify the church (hold it harmless) for any losses stemming from the use of the provider's EFT system.
- Establish clear policies and procedures. For members who want to give electronically, use an authorization form and policy statement that clearly explains their obligations and how your church will handle their request to modify or terminate electronic giving.
- Review internal controls and insurance coverage. Although no case has been reported yet, an electronic giving program could create an opportunity for embezzlement by a worker at the church. Therefore, make sure controls are in place so a second person is reviewing all electronic gifts, and include the program in the church's annual audit or financial review. Also, check with your insurance company to make sure appropriate employee dishonesty coverage is in place.

Insuring Your Church

Part of the risk management process is "risk financing," or making sure that funds are available to pay for any losses that might occur. Insurance is a key part of risk financing because, without it, your church will be responsible for paying for the entire cost of any damages or injuries that result from an accident or incident at church. Few churches have the financial resources to bear that responsibility on their own.

For example, a church without insurance that experiences a fire would have to come up with its own funds to rebuild the building. An uninsured church facing a claim of personal injury or an allegation of sexual misconduct would have to hire an attorney to defend itself against those allegations. In this way, insurance acts as a safeguard to your church's financial program. Insurance also protects against the claims of employee dishonesty, embezzlement, and theft discussed in this chapter.

But not all insurance is alike. Churches face certain risks that are not addressed in the typical insurance policy, even the typical commercial policy—things such as stained glass; spiritual counseling; organs; the pastor's personal property; newly acquired property; and equipment breakdown, including boilers, computers, and electrical equipment. Consider selecting an insurance company that includes coverage for these items in its commercial package policy.

In addition, churches face other risks that may need to be covered under separate parts or endorsements to their insurance policy, such as sexual misconduct liability, directors and officers liability, employment practices liability, non-owned and hired automobile liability, and employee benefits liability.

Because of their unique characteristics and exposures, churches should consider only insurance companies that specialize in church insurance and that offer these coverages in their commercial package policy. The company also should be financially secure.

It's important that churches consult with an insurance agent who is knowledgeable about the risks churches face and who works with an insurance company specializing in churches. In addition to assisting with the selection of appropriate insurance coverages and deductibles, your insurance agent also can help ensure that your church building is adequately insured to its value. Your agent should be able to assist your church with any questions you have and talk with you about the risk management ideas covered in this book.

Even after your church is insured, a periodic review of your church's insurance program with your insurance agent is strongly recommended to make sure that your church's finances and ministry are protected.

You'll Rest Easier

Yes, there are quite a few considerations, safeguards, policies, and procedures necessary to fully protect church finances. But once your Financial Safeguards Plan is developed and everyone is accustomed to following the procedures specified in the plan, your church's resources will be far more secure.

In addition to protecting your church with a plan, you may also enjoy some personal benefits as well. The next time you read about a case of theft or embezzlement at another church, you won't lose sleep worrying whether a similar crime could devastate your ministry.

If someone at your church is still not completely convinced that financial safeguards are essential, share this final example of an actual event—one of the most costly cases of church embezzlement within recent years.

$1.4 Million Allegedly Stolen

A former priest of a Catholic church in Connecticut pleaded guilty in federal court to charges that he stole hundreds of thousands of dollars from his wealthy parish, reported The Stamford Advocate in 2007.

According to the article, the priest, who had been at the church from 1991 to 2006 when he resigned, admitted he funneled church donations into two secret bank accounts, and then used the money for personal expenses. Despite his admission of guilt, the pastor disputed the amount of money that was taken.

An audit was commissioned and found that the priest had spent $1.4 million in church funds on luxuries such as a condominium, limousine rides, airline tickets, Giorgio Armani clothing, and dinners at upscale restaurants. As part of a plea agreement, the priest faced up to 10 years in prison and as much as $250,000 in fines as he awaited his sentence.

Chapter 7

Employee and Volunteer Safety

In 2005, a pastor was preparing to baptize a woman as about 800 congregation members watched during a Sunday service. According to witnesses, when he stepped into the water of the church's baptistery, he reached out and grabbed a corded microphone, which produced a fatal electric shock.

During a church workday, a 50-year-old volunteer was using a ladder to paint basketball support poles at a church's recreational center. Apparently, the woman set the ladder on an uneven surface. While she was at the top of the ladder, her weight caused it to fall, and she fractured her ankle in several places upon hitting the ground. Three weeks later, the woman died from a pulmonary embolism related to her ankle surgery.

A 42-year-old church worker was in the ceiling of the sanctuary to repair heating ducts when he accidentally stepped on a section of drywall that was not reinforced. The worker fell through the ceiling and landed on the sanctuary floor. He was transported to the hospital by ambulance and later died from injuries to his head.

Protecting the People Who Work at Your Church

Initially, when churches become motivated to develop safety and security (risk management) programs, one of the first priorities might be to protect innocent children from sexual abuse or seniors from slips, trips, and falls. Or the number one concern could be to address major facility risks such as an accidental fire, arson, burglary, or vandalism. While minimizing high-profile risks should be a top priority, an equally important aspect of risk management is the need to safeguard the employees and volunteers who work at your church.

As the three incidents described in the opening of this chapter illustrate, a church accident can be devastating. Granted, these types of tragedies are somewhat rare. But serious or even fatal accidents can easily take place at any church, especially if there are no policies and procedures in place for worker safety.

The reality is, church employees and volunteers such as pastors, office personnel, custodians, child care workers, youth pastors, and other staff members are frequently exposed to a wide variety of hazards. Whether those hazards are obvious (such as working on ladders and using power equipment) or more subtle (such as lifting objects or typing at a computer for an extended period of time), many typical workplace activities can cause minor, severe, or debilitating injuries. Therefore, showing you how to ensure the safety and personal health of church employees and volunteers is the goal of this chapter.

Additional Risk Management Concerns

Along with discussing how to enhance staff safety, this chapter will also cover equally important risk management topics that are closely related to employees and volunteers. These include workers' compensation risks; claims and lawsuits stemming from allegations of wrongful employment practices; and risks associated with religious counseling, mission trips, board member actions, food preparation, and ushers' responsibilities.

Workers' Compensation Risks

An important issue related to employee safety is the need to minimize the church's exposure to workers' compensation claims and costly lawsuits that can arise from staff injuries.

Workers' compensation insurance provides benefits for health care costs and lost wages to qualified employees and their dependents if any employee suffers a work-related injury or disease. Workers' compensation insurance can cover the following:

- loss of limbs
- work-related diseases, such as emphysema
- work-related injuries, such as those caused by repetitive motion
- medical treatment
- rehabilitation necessary for the injured worker to return to work
- lost wages (up to two-thirds of the employee's salary)
- death
- liability insurance for lawsuits filed by injured employees

Do You Really Need Workers' Compensation Insurance?

At this writing, in every state except Texas, workers' compensation insurance is legally mandated, and nonprofit organizations, including churches, are usually not exempt from the requirements. Therefore, if your organization does not carry workers' compensation insurance (and is required to do so), the organization could face financial or legal penalties. What's more, even if workers' compensation coverage is not required, your organization may still be held liable for lost wages and other costs stemming from a job-related injury.

To illustrate a common scenario, what if your church's maintenance man injured his back, leaving him unable to work? Unless your church carries the proper insurance coverage, an incident such as this can have serious financial consequences for the church. Depending on the severity of the worker's injury, the church may have to pay tens of thousands of dollars or more to cover the cost of lost wages, rehabilitation, and medical services.

The general liability coverage in a standard church insurance policy typically does not cover an employee injury. What's more, if your church is sued by the injured party, general liability coverage may not be sufficient to pay the costs.

For an extra level of protection, workers' compensation insurance—also known as workers' comp—can be purchased as an "add-on" coverage to your church's existing policy.

Regulations vary from state to state, but most states have a no-fault system, meaning that injured employees do not have to prove the work-related injury was someone else's fault in order to receive workers' compensation benefits for an on-the-job injury.

Talk with your insurance agent and/or an attorney to determine what level of workers' compensation coverage is appropriate for your church.

The Risk of Injury Increases With Volunteers

Churches must and should rely on volunteers to complete a wide variety of tasks. Volunteer work is intrinsic to a believer's calling as a person of faith. Nevertheless, it's essential to recognize that even though volunteers often have great intentions, certain individuals may overestimate their physical abilities, work beyond their level of expertise, or lack sufficient training in safety precautions. This is why volunteers are especially vulnerable to accidents and injuries.

The increased risk of volunteer injuries is another reason to develop policies and procedures to keep everyone safe. For reference, a "Safety Program Checklist" is available in the *SafeChurch Resource Packet* (free for download at www.safechurch .com). We encourage you to use and modify the checklist as needed.

Allegations of Wrongful Employment Practices

Any employer—including your church—can be sued by employees and prospective employees for allegations of wrongful employment practices. Allegations of discrimination, wrongful termination, sexual harassment, failure to hire or promote, and unfair performance evaluations are just a few examples of such lawsuits.

Employment-related risks are among some of the most potentially devastating exposures that a church of any size can face. Not only can an employment practices liability lawsuit cause financial misfortune, but it can also tarnish or severely damage an organization's reputation.

Most standard church insurance policies do not contain coverage for employment practices liability claims. As a result, churches should also consider carrying employment practices liability (EPL) insurance coverage. Again, consultation with an attorney and insurance professional is advised.

To help your church identify risks and issues related to employees and volunteers, ask your church leaders and Church Safety and Security (CSS) Team to complete the "Employee/Volunteer Risk Management Survey," available in the *SafeChurch Resource Packet* (downloadable for free at www.safechurch.com).

Safeguarding Those Who Serve

As mentioned in this chapter's introduction, the number one goal of a risk management program for employees and volunteers is to keep them safe. Employee safety is important not only because your church cares about its people but also because it makes good economic sense.

For instance, what happens if an employee such as a custodian or administrative assistant suffers from an injury and cannot work at your church for an extended period of time? Typically, a replacement worker will need to be found. This may take some time and effort, so the injured worker's hours are lost when he or she is not on duty, and the person in charge of finding a replacement loses hours as well. In addition, when a replacement worker is hired, he or she will have to be paid wages.

Also, as stated earlier, it's critical to minimize costly workers' compensation claims. In most states, your church could be legally responsible to provide wage replacement benefits as long as a worker is totally or partially disabled. Additionally, as an employer, your church must provide medical care to injured workers (at no cost to them) for restoration to their former physical condition. Even if you have workers' compensation insurance, any accident that occurs could potentially increase your insurance premiums. These are just a few of the pragmatic reasons churches are much better off when they strive to keep workers as healthy and safe as possible.

Steps to Prevent Injures and Minimize Employee Claims

1. **Hire the right person for the job.** It might sound overly simplistic, but it's extremely important to hire employees who are qualified and physically able to perform their jobs. Injuries often occur because an employee performs a task he or she is not fit to do. Two key steps help prevent this from occurring right from the start: a written job description and a health assessment.

2. **Provide a written job description.** A job description is essential for every position within the church. The document should include a general description of the job along with a list of the physical requirements, responsibilities, essential functions, and activities that must be performed by the employee. Estimated hours for activities should be included as well.

   A job description can be shared with a prospective employee during the application process so he or she understands the requirements of the job. The job description should also be used when evaluating potential employees to determine if they have the necessary skills and physical abilities for the position. Once an employee is hired, the job description should be signed by the employee and employer and maintained in a personnel file.

   During performance evaluations, supervisors can use the job description to counsel employees in areas where improvement is needed. In addition, if an employee suffers an injury or illness and needs to take medical leave, the job description may be used by a physician to determine when the employee can return to work in a customary manner, or with light duty, modified duty, alternate duty, or with job modifications. (Please see the discussion of "return-to-work programs" later in this section.)

3. **Provide a pre-employment health assessment.** When you hire a new employee, particularly for labor-intensive positions such as custodian, maintenance worker, or day-care worker, it is extremely helpful if the candidate is examined by a physician to determine if there are any health concerns. To take this important step, the church should provide a post-offer pre-employment health assessment. This physical is needed to obtain and document baseline information about pre-existing conditions in the event of a later injury and/ or workers' compensation claim. The physical will also help determine if a medical condition exists that will harm the individual or other employees. According to the Americans with Disabilities Act (ADA) of 1990 health assessments can be performed after a job has been offered (post-offer).

The employee's written job description will be needed for the health assessment, and a Post-Offer Pre-Employment Health Assessment form should be completed by the physician and church. (This form is included in the *SafeChurch Resource Packet*, which you may download from www .safechurch.com.)

4. **Conduct safety meetings with employees.** To keep safety issues and proper procedures fresh in the minds of employees, be sure to conduct regular (at least quarterly) safety meetings with staff members. Or discuss various safety topics during regular staff meetings once each month. Safety meetings are an easy and effective way to help prevent injuries or keep injury rates low. They also show employees how much the church cares about their health and well-being.

5. **Offer a return-to-work program.** If an injured employee is out for an extended period of time, an already sad situation only becomes worse. From an economic standpoint, lost-time injuries are the most expensive injuries, and the costs increase every day the injured employee is unable to work. Work-related injuries also increase the church's workers' compensation insurance premiums. In addition, studies also show that the longer workers are away from their jobs, the less likely they will ever return. These are key reasons it's so important for the church to offer a modified return-to-work program.

The primary goal of a modified return-to-work program is to return injured workers as soon as possible to their original jobs at either full duty or in a temporary assignment.

If an injured worker cannot return to his or her original job at full capacity, a modified return-to-work program provides temporary transitional duty to an injured employee who is still able to work but may have some restrictions.

Studies have shown that the earlier injured employees are permitted to return to work, the faster and better they will heal and recover.

A modified return-to-work program offers the following advantages for employees:

- It provides a sense of security and reduces concerns about continued employment.
- Injured workers remain active and productive, which reinforces feelings of self-worth.
- The employee retains benefits, retirement, and seniority.
- It minimizes pain and suffering and promotes physical health.
- Injured workers and their families experience less disruption in their lives.

Program advantages for churches include the following:

- A modified return-to-work program minimizes insurance costs for workers' compensation, medical, and disability claims.
- It helps retain skilled and experienced employees.
- It saves on costs for substitute employees' wages, as well as for hiring and retraining expenses.
- It reinforces the church's concern for injured workers, promoting staff morale and feelings of security.
- Co-workers are less likely to perform extra duties to make up for an absent employee.
- It reduces the potential for fraud. In certain situations, an employee might view medical leave as a vacation. Return-to-work programs demonstrate that getting injured does not mean getting out of work.

A policy statement like the following should be written and posted in an easily accessible place.

Sample Policy Statement

[Church name] is committed to providing a safe workplace for our employees. Preventing work-related illness and injury is our primary concern.

Our early return-to-work program provides opportunities for an employee who is injured on the job to return to work at full duty. If the injured worker is not physically capable of returning to full duty, the program provides opportunities for the worker to perform his or her regular job with modifications or, when available, to perform alternate temporary work that meets the injured worker's physical capabilities.

_____

Signature of Church Leader

_____

Date

Working to Enhance Staff Safety

As one of the largest Baptist churches in the state of Oklahoma, Henderson Hills Baptist has developed a wide variety of safety and security programs to protect its members, employees, and facilities. A few examples include a security staff, a video camera surveillance system, child abuse prevention training, and background checks for every employee.

When it comes to managing the church's large staff, Henderson Hills can serve as a role model for other churches. According to Kevin Nicolin, associate pastor of administration, the church has a comprehensive human resources program that includes a policy and procedures manual for all employees, written job descriptions for every position, and performance evaluations two times each year.

Nicolin is well aware that accidents can easily happen. For instance, after a recent snowfall, two employees decided to go sledding on the property during their break, and one man injured tendons in his foot and ankle, leaving him unable to work. Another accident occurred when a female custodian was vacuuming, tripped on a rope divider, and hurt her wrist.

"Fortunately, those were fairly minor injuries," Nicolin recalled. "So the worst part was the loss of man-hours. We had to scramble to get replacement workers, which obviously cost us time and money."

To help prevent future accidents and injuries, Nicolin is setting aside time during regular staff meetings to discuss various safety topics. "Most of it is really just common sense," Nicolin said, "but I think it's important for us to keep reminding our people about proper procedures for lifting, working with ladders, power tools, and things of that nature. Hopefully, our safety meetings will help avoid more injuries."

Preventing Maintenance Injuries

Some of the most frequent and common injuries happen to employees and volunteers who are performing general maintenance at church facilities. Every task—climbing a ladder to paint, changing a light bulb, unloading a delivery, using power tools to make a repair, cleaning with chemicals, or mowing the grass—can lead to both minor and severe injuries if something goes wrong.

Not every maintenance injury can be prevented. But by taking the proper precautions, such as conducting regular inspections, training and supervising workers, and posting safety reminders, many accidents can be avoided or minimized.

The Most Common Risks

It would be unrealistic for this book to cover every possible accident or injury scenario that can occur at a church. However, based on the most frequent and severe workers' compensation claims that are filed, there are a number of concerns that are especially important for churches to address and stress in worker safety training. They include the following:

- back injury prevention
- ladder fall prevention
- repetitive motion injury prevention
- slip and fall injury prevention (This topic is covered in Chapter 5; the principles also apply to worker safety.)

Back injury prevention—Back injuries account for one-third of all on-the-job injuries. Any work-related activities that require heavy lifting, repeated lifting, or bending or twisting of the back can increase the risk of back pain and injuries. For example, child care workers who must bend to pick up infants or squat down to a child's eye level may be prone to back injuries. Custodians, maintenance workers, and volunteers who are lifting any type of object can be injured as well. Many back injuries also occur on field trips and retreats when participants engage in rigorous activities such as skiing, snowboarding, sledding, or playing softball or other sports. (Refer to "Preventing Back Injuries" in the *SafeChurch Resource Packet*—free for download at www.safechurch.com—for procedures and policies to prevent back injuries.)

Ladder fall prevention—Every year, more than 500,000 people are treated for injuries resulting from ladder falls. Some accidents even result in death. All it takes for someone to end up in the emergency room is a simple mistake, loss of balance, slip, or a ladder that breaks. At religious facilities, uniquely shaped roofs and taller ceiling heights increase the dangers of working on ladders. Risks also increase if volunteers or employees unfamiliar with proper safety precautions use ladders. (See "Ladder Safety Procedures" in the *SafeChurch Resource Packet,* free for download at www.safechurch.com.)

Computer workstation safety and ergonomics—An office may seem like a safe place to work. But everyone who spends extended periods of time sitting at a computer workstation runs the risk of developing a variety of musculoskeletal disorders (MSDs). In fact, carpal tunnel syndrome is the leading MSD cause for taking time off from work. To help prevent unnecessary MSD injuries to workers, churches are strongly advised to evaluate all computer workstations and instruct workers on proper procedures and techniques. For instance, maintaining a neutral body position is key. A neutral position reduces stress and strain on the muscles, tendons, and skeletal system and minimizes the risk of developing MSDs.

Maintain a Neutral Body Posture at Computer Workstations

- Place the keyboard directly in front of you.
- Your shoulders should be relaxed and your elbows close to your body.
- Your wrists should be straight and in line with your forearms.
- Put the monitor directly in front of you and at least 20 inches away. The top line of the screen should be at or below eye level.
- Keep your head level or bent slightly forward and balanced in line with the torso.
- Feet should be fully supported by the floor or a footrest.
- Your back must be fully supported with appropriate lumbar support.
- Thighs and hips should be supported by a well-padded seat and should be generally parallel to the floor.
- Knees should be about the same height as the hips with the feet slightly forward.
- Keep the mouse/pointer close to the keyboard.
- Take breaks regularly.

Other work environment safety concerns—Adjust lighting to reduce glare on computer screens, ensure proper ventilation and air quality for worker comfort and health, and provide telecommunications equipment that eliminates awkward movement. See the "Safer Work Space Worksheet" in the *SafeChurch Resource Packet* (free for download at www.safechurch.com) for more details on setting up a safe work space.

Establish an Injury and Illness Prevention Program

Ultimately, one of the best and most professional ways to prevent job-related injuries, illnesses, and workers' compensation claims is to establish a comprehensive Injury and Illness Prevention Program (IIPP). This will help create a culture of safety throughout the church that involves everyone from employees and supervisors to CSS Team members.

Here are highlights of a typical IIPP:

- responsibilities of the safety committee, a coordinator, and staff members
- steps to identify workplace hazards with regular inspections and notification by staff
- correcting workplace hazards
- investigating injuries and illnesses
- employee health and safety training
- compliance issues
- record keeping
- essential forms for reporting hazards, safety committee documentation, safety inspection reports, workers' compensation reports, witness reports, safety training and attendance records

Safety issues, injuries, hazards, and corrective actions are frequently addressed by churches *after* a problem occurs. But with an IIPP and a commitment to making the program an ongoing effort, employees will stay safer and the church will greatly reduce its exposure to risks such as workers' compensation claims and costs associated with accidents and illnesses.

Protecting the Church Against Employment Practices Liability

Another important risk churches need to address is potential allegations of wrongful employment practices made by staff members and prospective employees. If such allegations are made, the church can be sued and found liable in court, and the judgment amount could be financially devastating.

Even if your church did nothing wrong and is not found legally liable, the fees to hire an attorney and defend the church against the suit could cost tens of thousands of dollars or more. The following are just a few examples of employment practices that have resulted in costly lawsuits. The names of the claimants and the organizations have been changed to protect their privacy.

Custodian sues church. John, who was a very likable fellow, had been a custodian at a Methodist church for a little more than a year. During his first six months, he came to work on time and performed his duties quite well. However, for the following eight months, John seemed to become lackadaisical about his job and said he was having family problems. He often arrived at the church several hours late, called in sick, or did not show up at all. While on the job, he failed to perform many of the tasks that were asked of him.

During his last two performance reviews, John's supervisor felt sorry for him, overlooked his poor work habits, and gave him favorable reviews. After that, John's attendance and efforts deteriorated further, and the church felt it had no choice but to let him go. John later filed a lawsuit against the church and claimed he was fired because he was overweight. The court decided in John's favor and awarded him $65,000 for wrongful termination.

Job applicant claims discrimination. A Presbyterian church located in an affluent neighborhood was in need of a nursery school assistant. The church placed a "help wanted" ad in the local paper, and eight people applied, including 23-year-old Juanita. When she completed her application for the job, it was apparent she had no previous experience working with children, but the church decided to interview her anyway. During the course of the interview, a church representative asked Juanita if she would be comfortable working at the church, and she replied: "Why, because I'm African American?" The interviewer explained that that was not the reason for the question. Rather, the question had been asked because Juanita had never worked in a church setting before. But Juanita still seemed irritated for the remainder of the interview.

As a courtesy, the church sent Juanita a thank you letter after the interview and ended up hiring a different woman with 12 years of preschool teaching experience. Two weeks later, an attorney for Juanita filed a lawsuit against the church for discriminatory hiring practices. The case was eventually settled out of court for $30,000, and the church ended up spending $22,000 on legal fees.

Lawsuits Can Come out of Nowhere

You might find it hard to believe that one of your own staff members or someone applying for a job would even consider suing the church. But given today's more litigious society, the harsh reality is that employment practice claims are one of the most common reasons that lawsuits are filed against churches. Here are a number of the situations that can create employment practices liability for a church:

- an alleged failure to hire or promote
- unjust demotion
- discriminatory slurs or comments
- termination
- unfair performance evaluations
- statements made by hiring personnel that could be understood as false promises of permanent employment
- claims of discrimination based on age, race, color, sex, national origin, religion, or disability
- failure to follow rules outlined by the Americans with Disabilities Act (ADA)
- failure to follow rules outlined by the Civil Rights Act of 1991
- situations in which an employee's work environment becomes so hostile that he or she feels forced to resign to protect financial, physical, or emotional well-being
- unwelcome sexual advances
- requests for sexual favors
- verbal, visual, or physical conduct of a sexual nature that is implied or presented as a condition of employment or used as a basis for employment discussions
- a work environment that interferes with job performance or creates an intimidating, hostile, or offensive situation

It's also important to note that the more full-time and part-time workers your church employs, the greater the risk of employment practices liability.

Could It Really Happen at Your Church?

It goes without saying that your church would never intentionally discriminate against someone, terminate an employee without just cause, allow sexual harassment to occur, or knowingly break an employment law. But what if a staff member (or job applicant) believes—whether justified or not—that he or she has been wronged in some way? That's all it takes for the person to contact an attorney and file a lawsuit.

So yes, allegations of wrongful employment practices can easily happen at any church. That's why it's critical to take steps to prevent allegations from occurring in the first place. And if an allegation is made, the church must be able to document and prove that either the incident did not occur or the church was not liable for the situation.

How Can Your Church Protect Itself?

The best solution is to develop a basic yet formalized human resources (HR) program with proper documentation, policies, and procedures. This will help ensure that all job applicants and employees are treated equally and consistently. Without an HR program in place, your church is leaving itself open to a wide variety of lawsuits stemming from employment relationships.

In addition to protecting the church from lawsuits, an HR program will help make sure your church hires and retains the best person for every job. Employees will have a better understanding of the church's expectations, requirements, policies, and procedures. The church can communicate a no-tolerance policy for sexual harassment. Job performance can be evaluated and improved. And should it become necessary to discipline or terminate an employee, an HR program will further protect the church from liability.

Also, before terminating any employee, it's important that your church consult with its employment attorney. It's better to pay the expense of a consultation now than to suffer the heartache and strain of an employment-related lawsuit down the road.

By creating the essential elements of an HR program and following the procedures, your church will be able to treat all employees equally, consistently, and without the appearance of bias or discrimination. Having the proper documentation in place is also essential if you ever need to defend the church against an allegation that results in a lawsuit.

If developing an HR program at your church sounds difficult or time-consuming, cast those thoughts aside. See "Creating an HR Program" on page 116.

Employee conduct standards—As employers, churches often seek to require or prohibit certain conduct by their employees both on and off the job. A common example is a church that discovers one of its employees is engaged in an extramarital affair and that seeks to terminate the person's employment because of it. Without having clearly notified the employee in advance regarding what is expected of him or her—and without applying its standards in a consistent and evenhanded manner—the church could be in a precarious legal position if the employee were to sue.

Points Worth Considering

- Put your church's employee conduct policy in writing, and include it in the employee handbook or other document that the employee will receive and acknowledge in writing.
- When writing the employee conduct policy, base it on theological or scriptural grounds. A policy based on religious grounds is less likely to be scrutinized by a court than a secular or nonreligious one.
- Have your employee conduct policy reviewed by a local employment attorney to make sure that it will stand up under federal, state, and local law.
- Once your policy is in place, apply it consistently. For example, if you terminate an unmarried female employee who becomes pregnant but do nothing about an unmarried male employee's sexual relationships, you are opening your church to charges that the firing was a pretext for gender discrimination.

Which employees might sue? When your church is evaluating risks related to employment practices, it's helpful to know that from a legal standpoint, there are two basic categories of employees: ministerial or pastoral employees and nonministerial employees.

For the first category of employees (ministerial or pastoral), the "ministerial exception" to federal employment laws generally prohibits courts from getting involved in employment disputes between churches and their clergy due to the First Amendment's guarantee of religious freedom. However, churches should still be concerned because courts are becoming increasingly involved in such disputes. For example, several courts have recently been involved in sexual harassment cases involving clergy, despite the ministerial exception.

When it comes to the second category of employees (nonministerial), there are even more reasons to be concerned. Basically, there are no restrictions for these employees to bring an employment lawsuit or claim against the church. Lawsuits are frequently filed by individuals in manual labor positions and by employees who work in preschool and school-related operations at churches.

Consider employment practices liability insurance. To fully protect your organization from lawsuits stemming from employment relationships, churches should strongly consider purchasing employment practices liability (EPL) insurance. An EPL policy is a separate coverage from a church's standard property and liability protection. With EPL insurance, the church will be covered if any claims are made by employees or job applicants for wrongful employment practices by the pastor or church. Most EPL insurance policies also cover the legal costs of hiring an attorney to defend the church. Without EPL insurance, even if an employment claim is without merit and ultimately dismissed, the church will be responsible for hiring and paying for an attorney to defend itself in the case. Some insurance companies require churches to carry directors, officers, and trustees liability insurance in order to qualify for EPL coverage, so be sure to consult with an insurance professional about the options available for your church.

Additional Staff-Related Risks

According to the records of GuideOne Insurance, in 20 percent of sexual misconduct claims filed against churches, the alleged victims are adults. Of those incidents, the overwhelming majority take place in a counseling setting.

Religious Counseling Concerns

If one or more of your church staff provide counseling to adults, it's critical to be aware of the risks to which your church and counselor may be exposed. Allegations against those who provide religious counseling can take many forms, including negligent counseling, clergy malpractice, abuse of authority, breach of fiduciary duty, undue influence, breach of confidentiality, alienation of affection, sexual battery, and defamation. Whether these types of allegations are true or unfounded, a costly lawsuit against the church is likely to result. (To protect your church and counselors from allegations of misconduct in a counseling setting, implement the "Counseling Misconduct Safeguards" in the *SafeChurch Resource Packet* (free for download at www.safechurch.com).

Although taking the proper precautions when counseling members can reduce risk for the church and counselor, there is always a chance that sexual misconduct may still occur. The emotional toll from such an incident can be heartbreaking for those involved, and the legal costs can be equally devastating if the church is sued. That's why it's important to consider carrying sexual misconduct liability insurance, which is separate coverage from the church's standard insurance policy. Sexual misconduct insurance covers incidents of both child molestation and adult victimization. By purchasing sexual misconduct coverage, the organization will be protected from legal liability, including defense costs, arising from acts of sexual misconduct by a counselor, whether the counselor is an employee or volunteer.

Mission Trips

Building a church in Mexico, assisting with disaster relief, and delivering vaccines in Africa are just a few of the many mission trips that churches take each year.

As opportunities to show compassion and generosity, mission trips are extremely rewarding. Nevertheless, church leaders must also recognize that such trips can expose the organization, its employees, and volunteers to a wide variety of unique and dangerous risks, particularly if the group is traveling abroad.

Mission Trip Risks

- injury or serious illness
- vehicle accident
- abduction or kidnapping
- robbery or assault
- sexual abuse of a minor
- civil war, political unrest, and terrorism
- hurricane, flood, and other natural disasters
- lawsuit filed against the church

Naturally, the risks associated with a mission trip will vary depending on where the group is going and the type of volunteer work they will be performing. But if your church is organizing a mission, leaders of the church are responsible for considering the risks, exercising good judgment, and taking the proper precautions. In the *SafeChurch Resource Packet* (free for download at www.safechurch.com), a "Mission Trip Planning Worksheet" lists important actions, issues, and steps that can help minimize the risks of mission trips. Important considerations should include (1) establishing a written policy for mission trips, (2) getting travel security information, (3) careful planning and preparation for the trip, (4) health issues, (5) participant training, and (5) arrangement of safe land travel.

There are, of course, many other factors to consider when organizing a mission, but with careful planning, preparation, and training, your church can further enhance the safety of its mission group and protect it from unnecessary risk.

Church Boards May Face Unforeseen Risks

Chances are, your church board members are competent, trustworthy, and wise. But what if a poor decision is made regarding church finances or an employment matter? Could a building project exceed its budget? What if funds are lost because of an investment decision? These situations can easily occur and can trigger a costly liability lawsuit. In addition, church board members have been personally sued over decisions made by their church boards such as continuing to use 15-passenger vans and failing to implement safeguards to protect the church's children.

While federal law provides limited immunity from liability for uncompensated members of nonprofit boards in certain circumstances, church and board members can incur substantial costs in defending themselves from lawsuits. And if the court finds either party legally liable for damages, the judgment amount could be devastating. Church leaders could even be forced to pay large sums out of their own pockets.

Legal Concerns Are Real

Consider these two scenarios:

- The church wants to build an addition to its facility. The board of directors requests competitive bids from several local contractors and decides to award the project to the lowest bidder. Later, it's learned that a board member's brother-in-law works for the contractor who won the project. The other contractors sue the church and board of directors, alleging a conflict of interest.
- In accordance with the will of an elderly widow, a large donation is made to the church with the stipulation that the funds be used to pay for new pews in the sanctuary. One year later, the donor's son visits the church and learns the pews have not been purchased and the money was used for another purpose. In anger, he files a lawsuit against the board of directors.

The following is a list of the types of situations that can create liability for church boards and the organization:

- using funds that are budgeted or donated to the church in a way that was not originally intended or agreed upon
- committing oversights and errors in conducting a major building program
- discriminating in membership standards
- failing to preserve qualifications for tax exemption of the nonprofit organization (These regulations can be highly complex.)
- exceeding the authority granted by the church's charter or bylaws
- breaching provisions of an employee contract
- failing to maintain adequate financial records
- failing to act upon an apparent conflict of interest involving a board member
- failing to properly administer employee benefits
- failing to pursue an insurance claim
- failing to maintain standards for denominational affiliation of clergy
- failing to take effective steps to remove unsatisfactory personnel
- experiencing general conflict of interest
- displaying a lack of good judgment, diligence, or good faith
- making unauthorized or imprudent loans or investments

To help protect board members, a number of precautions should be taken.

Develop written job descriptions. Like other church staff, board members should be keenly aware of their responsibilities, duties, and obligations. If board members can be held legally liable for their actions, they should be made aware of the potential risk.

Provide training. It is the rare church that provides training to its incoming board members. Look for resources that your church can provide to its board. Denominational resources are available in certain denominations to assist local church board members in their work. Other nonprofit resource organizations, such as the Christian Management Association, can also be a resource for your board members.

Consult with an attorney. To determine what types of risks board members might face, consult with an attorney who has experience in the area of nonprofit board members' liability/immunity in your state. Also check into your church's corporate documents, such as its articles of incorporation and bylaws, to determine what they say regarding board members. You may want to discuss with the church's attorney the concept of indemnification of board members.

Purchase directors, officers, and trustees liability insurance. One of the most effective ways to protect board members is to purchase directors, officers, and trustees liability insurance, which is commonly referred to as D&O (Directors and Officers) coverage. As a separate coverage from the church's standard insurance policy, typical D&O insurance is designed to provide coverage for wrongful acts of directors, officers, trustees, business administrators, and pastors/ministers. The policy will pay for legal costs and court judgments if the church has no prior knowledge of the alleged wrongful act.

The level of protection and specific situations that are covered by D&O insurance will vary depending on the company that provides it. So be sure to discuss the policy details with a church insurance professional. If you work with an insurer that specializes in churches, you may find that D&O coverage is both affordable and easily obtained.

Remember that you have an obligation to protect leaders. Your church's board members and other leaders provide invaluable service to the organization, often as volunteers with no compensation. Therefore, they deserve to be protected—especially from situations over which they have no control. As you are developing your risk management program for employees and volunteers, be sure to include safeguards for the board, so that they, too, can feel secure.

Food Safety

For just about any type of food that's served at your church—snacks for Sunday school, potluck dinners, pancake breakfasts, or meals for any event—you probably have numerous volunteers working in the church kitchen. You know those people have hearts of gold, work hard, and prepare food with loving care.

But what if an oversight or accident caused a massive case of food poisoning?

Or something even more bizarre could occur. At one church, a volunteer accidentally poured cleaning solution into a punch bowl. At another church, a young man who was angry with his sister put an illegal drug in the brownies she took to church. Fortunately, these incidents were caught before anyone was seriously harmed, but the outcomes could have been deadly.

To minimize food risks, be sure the people who work in your kitchen receive training and reminders about proper preparation, serving, and storing of food items. It's also wise to post procedures and tips for proper preparation. See "Proper Food Handling" in the *SafeChurch Resource Packet* (free for download at www .safechurch.com) for food safety procedures and tips.

The Role of the Usher

More and more churches are expanding the roles that ushers play. In addition to handing out bulletins and collecting offerings, many ushers are being asked to take responsibility for basic security and to serve as first responders in medical emergencies. While ushers can be great assets in these capacities, care must also be taken to ensure that ushers stay safe when performing their duties, especially if an urgent situation arises.

Enhancing Usher Safety

- Develop a church security plan and guidelines with defined roles for all staff, including ushers, greeters, and other front-line workers. Include in the plan a seating location for ushers, strategically stationed in both the front and rear of the sanctuary. Also develop lockdown procedures for areas of the church, communications, and an evacuation plan.
- Establish a method for quickly communicating issues of concern (such as a menacing person, weapon, or medical emergency) to appropriate church personnel, the security director, and authorities. Equip ushers and other personnel with walkie-talkies, two-way radios, pagers, and/ or cell phones.
- Maintain a no-tolerance policy for fights, squabbles, and other disruptions.
- Work with your local law enforcement agency to provide training for ushers and other front-line workers on topics such as violence identification and security methods.

- Openly discuss issues of concern, and train ushers to diffuse problems before they become incidents.
- Provide ushers with first-aid, CPR, and AED (defibrillator) training.
- In the event of an emergency, instruct ushers to call 911 or another designated emergency number.
- If there is a menacing person and an opportunity to keep the invader out, ushers should lock the doors or close off areas of the church.
- Ushers should not try to confront or stop a menacing person on their own. They should call 911 or church security personnel.
- When an offering needs to be transported or moved from one location to another, two unrelated adult ushers should do the job.
- Stress to ushers that their personal safety should always come first.

A Great Training Tip

Henderson Hills Baptist Church in Edmond, Oklahoma, hires a police officer to coordinate its security team and to schedule off-duty police officers to work at the church for various events. The lead officer also plays a vital role in training staff members.

"The officer we work with has been a huge asset for our security program," Kevin Nicolin, associate pastor of administration, said. "From time to time, we have him come in and brief our ushers, custodians, and other members of the staff on various security issues. The officer talks about typical situations the staff might encounter and discusses the best ways to handle them based on his personal experience. I would definitely suggest that other churches look into the possibility of getting a police officer to help them out with their training needs."

Best Intentions and Good Stewardship

Clearly, there are many forces at work that, despite your best intentions and sincere motives, can pose significant threats to your church and its members and staff. Those placed in a stewardship role over the church must consider themselves accountable to God and their authorities for how they handle those responsibilities.

But even more so, regardless of your role with the church, you can certainly appreciate the organization's moral responsibility to protect employees and volunteers. Obviously, they deserve the same level of concern, compassion, and safety precautions as every other member. After all, church employees and volunteers are a precious part of your ministry. They devote countless hours of service to the church, often for no compensation or for modest wages.

Creating an HR Program

We recommend creating the following documents as you develop the fundamental elements of your church's HR program. Once they're developed, it's critical to have them reviewed by an employment lawyer in your community to ensure that your HR program complies with federal, state, and local laws.

Job application form—When hiring employees, it's important to follow a formal and documented hiring process that starts with an employment/job application. This will give the church a snapshot of the candidate's qualifications, references, employment history, and other important information. Once the applicant has completed the application and the application has been reviewed, all qualified candidates should go through an interview process. These steps are essential to identify the most qualified people and eliminate individuals who may not have the appropriate skills or who may pose a risk to the church.

Job descriptions—As mentioned earlier in this chapter, job descriptions should be written for every position in the church.

Background check consent form—Prospective employees must provide written consent to have background checks performed. We strongly recommend background checks for all applicants. In fact, if the applicant will be working with children or youth or will be involved in church finances, a background check should be mandatory. A background check is more than just a reference check. It provides a search of public records to determine if the candidate has a criminal past. This is another important way to screen applicants and determine if there are any reasons they should not be hired. Knowing that a background check will be performed may also scare away sexual predators.

Reference check documentation form—The church should contact at least three references listed on a candidate's job application. At least one reference should be a past employer or a professional person or (if the candidate has not held a prior job) a teacher. This form should include appropriate questions to ask the references and areas to document their responses.

Employee handbook—Once an employee is hired, he or she should be required to read the church's employee handbook, which covers key employment policies on topics such as sick leave, employee conduct and grievances, anti-harassment, discrimination, and job-related injuries and illnesses.

Performance evaluation form—On a regular basis, a supervisor should provide each employee with a candid performance evaluation to identify strengths and weaknesses. At many churches, there is a tendency to provide glowing evaluations, even if an employee does not deserve them. Therefore, care should be taken to avoid overly positive evaluations in the event the employee is terminated in the future.

Performance improvement form—If an employee needs to make performance improvements, it's important to identify and document those areas so the employee understands what is expected. A plan of action should also be created with dates to achieve specific goals.

Chapter 8

Child and Youth Protection

Reflecting back on July 12, 2000, Pastor Ryan Peterson remembered how troubling his first day was at Mountainside Christian Church.* Located in a resort area of a Southeastern state, Mountainside had been operating without a pastor for several months before Pastor Peterson accepted the job and arrived in town.

"It was literally my first day at the church, and as I was unpacking boxes in the office, the church secretary pulled me aside and told me that a tragic story would be appearing in the local newspaper the next day," Pastor Peterson recalled. "A man who had recently been attending the church was being accused of molesting an 8-year-old boy. The perpetrator had met the boy and his family at our church, and after gaining their trust, offered to take the boy camping. That is when the abuse occurred."

Pastor Peterson recounted how the child molester had committed similar offenses in the past and was found guilty of his latest crime. The local court sentenced the man to four and a half years in prison, but after serving only six months, he was released and then he moved away to a large metro area.

"So very early on in my ministry here, it was obvious that we needed to be more cautious, proactive, and do everything that we could to keep our kids safe," Pastor Peterson said.

The pastor worked closely with the church's board of directors to establish a comprehensive child protection program. "One of the first things we did was walk through the church and identify 'danger zones'—secluded places where a

*The names of the pastor and church have been changed to protect their privacy.

predator might be able to take a child and abuse him or her without being seen," Peterson explained. To eliminate the danger zones, a number of steps were taken. Locks were installed on all closets, as well as on storage and utility rooms. And to increase visibility, windows were installed in many doors throughout the church, including classrooms, offices, and other areas. "Now all church activities are extremely visible, and people can't hide what they're doing."

The church also implemented a policy to conduct criminal background checks on everyone who works with children and youth. Personal references are required and checked as well. "The policy applies to all staff, volunteers, and church leaders, including me," Pastor Peterson said. "There are no exceptions, and not a single person has objected to doing this."

"We've gone on to enhance the safety and security of our building in many other ways, too," Pastor Peterson added. "But our kids have been the primary focus since I arrived. They really are our most precious resource, and we have to protect them to the best of our ability."

Unfortunately, there are countless similar examples in which children have been sexually abused at their churches. For instance, a church janitor coerced a 12-year-old boy onto an elevator, took him to the basement of the facility, and molested him. A church day-care director allowed her 17-year-old foster son to watch over the children. The teenager molested a 7-year-old girl when they were left alone. (Eventually, the church day care was forced to shut down because of the negative publicity.) And during a children's game of Flashlight Tag outside of a church, a 10-year-old boy molested a 7-year-old girl while isolated in an unlit area of an amphitheater.

Abuse Takes Many Forms

Along with the dangers of sexual misconduct, there are, of course, other types of child abuse, including neglect, physical abuse, and emotional abuse. While these are also very serious concerns and churches should be on the lookout for them, studies indicate that parents or guardians are usually responsible for most of these types of reported incidents.

Abuse Statistics

According to a "Child Maltreatment" study by the U.S. Department of Health and Human Services in 2006, among child victims of sexual abuse, 26.2 percent were abused by a parent, and 29.1 percent were abused by a relative other than a parent. The remaining 44.7 percent were abused by perpetrators not related to the children.

Since sexual abuse is one of the greatest risks churches face when dealing with minors, sexual misconduct prevention will be a primary focus of this chapter. What's more, steps to prevent sexual abuse can also help prevent other forms of abuse.

Safety Issues

In addition to discussing steps to minimize the risks of child sexual abuse, this chapter will also address the following safety issues related to children and youth ministries:

- Nursery Safety
- Playground Safety
- Recreational Activity Safety
- Youth Trip and Overnight Retreat Safety
- Computer and Internet Safety for Youth

Before moving on to look at specific safety issues related to children and youth, please ask your church leaders and Church Safety and Security (CSS) Team to take a moment to complete the "Child and Youth Risk Management Survey," provided in the *SafeChurch Resource Packet* (free for download at www .safechurch.com). Like the general surveys presented in previous chapters, this exercise will help you quickly identify key actions that are necessary to enhance safety and security.

Preventing Child Sexual Abuse

When you see the innocent faces of young children at your church, hear them laughing, singing, and playing, and watch them learn about the Bible with wonder and fascination, it's impossible to understand how any human being could ever be so cruel as to sexually abuse a child.

But as shepherds and protectors of our flocks, we have to recognize an unfortunate reality: Sex offenders will always exist in this world. They can strike in any church, regardless of its size, denomination, location, or socioeconomic makeup. Because of the enormous risks of sexual abuse, it's the responsibility of every church to put safeguards in place to protect the safety of children and youth.

After the highly publicized allegations of sexual abuse in Catholic churches that surfaced in the early 2000s, nearly everyone is aware that sexual misconduct can and does happen in religious settings. As other reports have also illustrated, sexual abuse occurs far too frequently in churches of all denominations.

Despite all the news about child sexual abuse, if your church has never experienced an allegation of sexual misconduct, it's easy to believe that it won't happen in your organization. But the truth is, if the proper safeguards are not in place, every youngster and church is vulnerable to an incident of sexual abuse. Even an allegation of sexual misconduct that has no merit can have a devastating impact on a church and the person who was falsely accused.

What's at Stake

Child sexual abuse is one of the most difficult topics for religious leaders and volunteers to discuss because it makes everyone uncomfortable. Yet there is simply too much at stake to avoid talking about the issue and taking action.

Just imagine—if a child is sexually abused while in the care of your church, you'll experience a nightmare of tragedy and sorrow that can last for years. Obviously, the victim and family members will suffer emotionally for the rest of their lives. Congregation members will be frightened, others will be angry, and a certain number may leave the church. Leaders of the church could be blamed for allowing the abuse to occur. And within the community, the church's reputation will be severely damaged by the negative publicity.

Adding further to the pain, if a lawsuit is filed against the church, which is frequently the case, the legal costs and court judgment could devastate the church financially. Some churches never recover from an incident of child molestation.

Truly faithful churches cannot conscientiously use hope, trust, and prayer as excuses for improper stewardship. Scripture emphasizes that faith must be accompanied by action. Steps simply must be taken to protect innocent lives, the reputations of your staff, and the future of your ministry.

Child Sexual Abuse Statistics

Estimates of child sexual abuse rates vary significantly from one source to another for a variety of reasons. For instance, experts believe that only about 10 percent of all child sexual abuse cases are reported to the police. Abuse may be underreported because victims are frightened, ashamed to reveal incidents, have repressed memories of abuse, or the families may not be willing to discuss the incident. The ways in which sexual abuse is defined may also affect the frequency of reports. Therefore, the following statistics should be viewed as estimates of a problem that is probably worse than the numbers indicate.

• According to substantiated cases by state and local child protective services, approximately 79,640 children were sexually abused in 2006.[1]

- Sexual abuse occurs in rural and metro areas, regardless of race, ethnic, or socioeconomic status. [2]
- Most children are abused by someone they know and trust. Approximately 60 percent of offenders are acquaintances of the victims, 26 percent are parents, and 14 percent are strangers. [3]
- In a typical year, GuideOne Insurance, one of America's largest church insurers, receives 10 to 15 sexual misconduct claims each month. Protestant churches account for 97 percent of these claims. [4]
- Approximately 1 percent of all churches in the United States report an incident of sexual misconduct each year. Since many cases go unreported, the actual frequency of abuse is believed to be higher. [5]

SOURCES:
[1] "2006 Child Maltreatment" study by the U.S. Department of Health and Human Services
[2] National Committee to Prevent Child Abuse
[3] *Sexual Assault of Young Children as Reported to Law Enforcement,* U.S. Department of Justice
[4] GuideOne Insurance 2007 statistics
[5] Ibid.

Sexual Abuse Defined

Most people have a pretty good guess about what kinds of terrible acts can occur when a child is sexually abused. But it's important for church staff and volunteers to have a clear understanding of how child sexual abuse is officially defined. Definitions of child sexual abuse vary from state to state but typically include the following:

- Any sexual act between an adult and a minor, or between two minors who are separated by at least four years of age.
- Any fondling, penetration, intercourse, exhibitionism, pornography, exposure to sexual acts or explicit materials, exploitation, and child prostitution.

While the examples just mentioned clearly fall into the category of abuse, other activities are not so clear. Depending on the background and sensitivities of the person involved, a hug or other genuine expression of affection may be perceived as an inappropriate act in the mind of the receiver. For that reason, those who work with children and youth need to be extra cautious about how their behavior may be perceived. Some churches go so far as to create detailed "touching guidelines" for their workers, specifying exactly how they may or may not touch children and youth at the church. While the wisdom of such detailed policies is left to the judgment of each church, consider these guiding principles:

- Any touching (such as hugging) must be age-appropriate and based on the need of the child, not the worker. For example, a college-age volunteer holding a 2-year-old who has fallen and skinned his knee would be appropriate, whereas the same volunteer hugging a high school–age youth group member of the opposite sex may not.
- Touching should never take place in isolated settings such as closed offices, classrooms, other nonpublic settings, or one-on-one situations.
- Touching should never take place on personal parts of the body such as private areas, except when following the church's diapering procedures.

Workers should at all times avoid the appearance of impropriety. By establishing appropriate boundaries and avoiding situations that could be misinterpreted by onlookers, church workers can help avoid allegations of abuse or inappropriate conduct.

Can You Spot a Child Molester?

To fully understand the need for safeguards at your church, it's helpful to understand a few disturbing facts about child molesters and why they frequently go unnoticed.

There is no single profile that can be applied to all child molesters. But experts who work with sex offenders say that molesters share a number of similar characteristics. For instance, preferential pedophiles seek out situations that allow them to interact with children, which makes churches a common target. Because of the trusting nature of churches, the need for volunteers, and a general lack of scrutiny, pedophiles can sometimes gain quick and easy access to children at houses of worship.

Other types of child sex offenders include situational molesters, who act on impulse if given the opportunity. Women sometimes commit sexual misconduct with minors. And another growing category of molesters includes older children who abuse younger children.

In general, though, the majority of child molesters are adult males who you might least suspect. They are usually dedicated, personable, respected, and well liked in the church, and appear to be "great with kids." Some are married with families of their own. But they are truly wolves in sheep's clothing. You might be an excellent judge of character, but you simply cannot identify molesters by their appearance or personalities. However, since child molesters are often repeat offenders, they may have a record of prior offenses, or they might have behaved suspiciously at other organizations.

What's more, child sex offenders may be able to conceal their crimes because victims of molestation are often reluctant to step forward. Young children who have been abused may not understand what happened. Offenders can sometimes convince their victim that he or she instigated the sexual contact and was the one at fault. Thus, victims may be afraid they'll get in trouble if they let anyone know about the abuse. Other victims may be too frightened or embarrassed or don't think anyone will believe them. Likewise, molesters frequently threaten, intimidate, and coerce their victims to remain silent.

Alleged Offenders at Churches

If you are a pastor or other church employee, we certainly do not want to cast a cloud of suspicion over your head. But according to the records of GuideOne Insurance, when sexual misconduct insurance claims are reported, the alleged offenders fall into four categories:

- Fifty-five percent are pastors and staff.
- Twenty percent are members or volunteers.
- Twenty percent are other minors.
- Fewer than 5 percent are strangers.

There is no precise way to determine how many of the alleged claims of sexual misconduct are with or without merit. Yet because of the frequency of allegations against pastors, staff, members, and volunteers, everyone at your church who works with children and youth must take special precautions to prevent abuse as well as avoid being falsely accused.

Developing a Child and Youth Protection Policy

Every church can keep its children and youth safer and more secure by developing and adopting a written Child and Youth Protection Policy, which is shared with employees, volunteers, congregation members, and job applicants. Naturally, everyone who works with children and youth must read the policy, understand it, and follow through with its implementation.

To assist churches in developing a Child and Youth Protection Policy, a sample policy template is included in the *SafeChurch Resource Packet* (free for download at www.safechurch.com).

In general, a Child and Youth Protection Policy should address the following topics:

- who will be able to work with children and youth
- how they will be selected and screened
- what safe practices will be followed
- how to respond to allegations

The following are highlighted recommendations for a Child and Youth Protection Policy. Please note that the terms *child* and *children* will be used to refer to all persons under the age of 18.

Proper Selection of People Who Work With Children

Most people who enjoy working with children have great intentions. But for a variety of reasons, there are certain individuals who simply should not be allowed to do so. Anyone who has a history of sexually abusing children should obviously be ruled out immediately. But histories of violence, crime, drug abuse, or mental illness are just a few more reasons that some individuals may pose a risk to children. That's why proper procedures for selecting and screening child workers are critical.

Require a Six-Month Waiting Period

Remember when we mentioned that sex offenders want to gain quick and easy access to children? A six-month rule can provide an effective deterrent to such individuals if they come to your church. As part of the Child and Youth Protection Policy, establish a six-month rule that requires all volunteers to be active in the life of the church for a minimum of six months before they can apply for a position that involves interacting with, supervising, instructing, or having occasional contact with children. This rule will also allow church leaders to more carefully evaluate all newcomers to determine their suitability for various positions.

Use Written Job Applications

Some churches may feel that a formal job application process is unnecessary, especially for volunteers. Or they may feel that when workers are needed quickly, certain procedures can be overlooked. But if an application process is not used, the church exposes itself and children to serious and unnecessary risks. Everyone who is interested in working with children should be required to complete and sign a written application form supplied by the church. Please see the *SafeChurch Resource Packet* (free for download at www.safechurch.com) for an example of a "Child/Youth Worker Application Form."

The application should request basic information from the candidate including previous experience working with children, previous church affiliation(s), references, employment information, and a disclosure of any previous criminal convictions. Once completed, the application should be kept confidential and on file in a secure location.

Conduct Personal Interviews

When a candidate appears to be qualified based on his or her application, one or more face-to-face interviews should be conducted by the church to further evaluate the candidate's qualifications and suitability for the job. An interview is another essential step in the selection process and can help determine whether the individual has the right type of personality, commitment, and demeanor to be worthy of the church's trust. If there are doubts or concerns about the candidate following the interview, the church will save valuable time if the process stops at this point. But if all goes well during the interview, the church can proceed with the additional steps in the screening process.

Check References and Document Responses

Reference checks are extremely important when selecting people who will work with children. A reference can provide candid information that is not available from any other source. So make sure the church's responsible parties contact at least two or three of the references listed on the job application, ask appropriate questions, and document the responses.

Also, instead of personal or family references, the candidate should provide references that are institutional in nature, preferably from organizations where he or she has worked with children in the past. When reference checks are completed and documented, the forms should be kept confidential and stored in a secure location.

Conduct Criminal Background Checks

Anyone who will work with children should be required to sign an authorization form that grants his or her permission for the church to conduct a national criminal background check. (A criminal background check is also recommended for all church employees, regardless of their positions.) Ideally, the authorization form should be completed during the application process. And if an individual declines to sign the authorization form, he or she should not be allowed to work with children.

Criminal background checks are especially important for those involved with the following:

- the church's school, preschool, or day-care center;
- overnight retreats or activities with minors;
- counseling of minors;
- mentoring programs with minors; and
- occasional one-on-one contact with minors, such as coaches of church-sponsored athletic teams and vehicle drivers.

Easy and Affordable Background Checks

Thanks to the Internet and a variety of online screening services, national criminal background checks are now easy and affordable for churches to conduct. Currently, there are hundreds of background screening vendors to choose from. When deciding on a background screening company, consider several factors in addition to price:

- available searches
- data availability in your state
- account setup process
- report format and delivery mechanism
- training and instruction provided
- availability of sample forms
- compliance with Fair Credit Reporting Act (FCRA) requirements
- customer service

If in doubt as to the value of such research, consider these statistics:

- According to one national criminal background search provider, 6 percent of the criminal background checks conducted for all types of industries reveal at least one criminal offense.
- 5.2 percent of the criminal background checks that GuideOne Insurance policyholders (primarily churches) conducted in a recent year revealed a criminal offense. In other words, one in 20 church background checks turned up a crime in the individual's past. These crimes included murder and rape as well as offenses involving children, such as sexual assault on a child and unlawful intercourse with a minor.

Also keep in mind that it's always best to conduct a national criminal background check and not just a check of your state's records. Research shows that over half of the convictions found in criminal background checks come from states other than the applicant's state of residence. Oftentimes, sexual offenders and other criminals move from one state to another, so a national check is necessary to identify any offenses that took place outside of your state.

What to Do If a Criminal Offense Is Identified

If a background check reveals the job applicant committed a criminal offense in the past and he or she did not disclose it in the job application, the applicant should be immediately disqualified. Likewise, if a conviction was for any offense involving children and/or violence, dishonesty, illegal substances, indecency, or any other conduct contrary to the church's mission, the individual should not be allowed to work with children.

One suggestion in deciding whether a certain criminal offense in someone's past should disqualify him or her from working with the children in your church is to check with the local school district or other youth-serving charities about what crimes disqualify applicants from working with children there. Then consider following their guidelines. In that way, your church will be bringing its practice in line with the community standard of care.

In certain situations, if church leaders proceed with great caution, hiring decisions can be made on a case-by-case basis with consideration for the circumstances surrounding the offense. However, it is usually best to put the safety of children first and err on the side of caution. As the following example illustrates, giving someone a second chance can be a grave mistake.

The Danger of a Second Chance

At a Presbyterian church, a youth minister was fired for having gay porno-graphic materials in his office. Later, the man was hired as a youth minister by a different church. At the second church, leaders knew about the man's past but decided to give him a second chance.

Over a period of several years at the second church, the new youth minis-ter showed gay pornographic videos to a number of adolescent boys. He also supplied them with alcohol and cigarettes and engaged in sex acts with at least two of the boys, who were 15 years of age. Liability lawsuits for sexual misconduct were filed against the youth minister and church, which resulted in court settlements costing hundreds of thousands of dollars.

The Bible teaches that there are high moral standards for people in leadership positions and that even with forgiveness being properly understood, an individual's past still should be weighed and carefully considered. While forgiveness, mercy, and grace are important concepts, it is equally important to understand the danger of affording second chances to individuals who have behaved inappropriately with children in the past. This is not to say that such individuals must be excluded from the life of the church entirely. Indeed, other ministry opportunities may be open to them, but working with the children and youth of the church should not be one of those options. Shepherds of the church must never create unnecessary risks for the children and youth entrusted to their care.

As this section has described, by developing a Child and Youth Protection Policy that requires a six-month waiting period, written job applications, personal interviews, reference checks, and criminal background searches, the church will be able to properly screen and select the best people to work with youngsters and keep them from harm.

Proper Supervision

Another important step in preventing child abuse, injuries, and accidents is to make sure that all activities involving children and youth are properly supervised. To achieve this goal, guidelines for supervision should be clearly described in your church's Child and Youth Protection Policy, and all workers should be required to adhere to the rules. We recommend the following guidelines:

The Two-Adult Rule

Ideally, two unrelated adult workers should be present when children are being supervised or instructed during programs and activities. This rule can significantly reduce the risk of child abuse as well as the potential for false accusations. Also, in the event of an injury or emergency, one adult will be able to assist the child while the other adult calls for help.

In certain situations, however, Sunday school or youth classes might have only one adult teacher during the classroom session. If it's not possible to have another adult present during a youth class, the door(s) to the classroom should remain open at all times and there should be no fewer than three students with the adult teacher. One minor and one adult should never be alone on the premises unless it's in a prearranged counseling situation, which a parent or guardian has approved. A consent form should be signed prior to any one-on-one counseling with a minor.

Maintain an Open-Door Policy and High Visibility

All activities involving children and youth should be highly visible to people outside the classroom. To maintain visibility, the doors of the classroom should always be left open unless glass windows are installed on the doors, next to the doors, or on walls of the classroom. Doors should never be locked while people are in the room.

Many older churches have greatly increased the visibility of their classrooms, child care areas, and pastors' offices by having windows retrofitted in doors and walls. The installation process is quite affordable and is an excellent investment for churches that want to increase safety and security.

Video camera monitoring systems in classrooms and child care areas are another option that quite a few churches are electing to use to enhance supervision. The cameras record all activities and provide an effective deterrent to inappropriate actions, and the recordings may be viewed at a later time if necessary.

Child Check-In / Checkout Procedures

For children who are younger than an age specified by your church (for example, less than 10 years old), we strongly recommend using formal child check-in/ checkout procedures.

Here is a basic yet effective approach to these procedures: The child is signed in by a parent or guardian who receives a "child check" similar to a claim check. Upon returning to pick up the child, the parent or guardian must present the child check in order to sign out and leave with the child. If a parent or guardian is unable to present the child check, a church leader must be contacted. The leader will then be responsible for making the decision to release the child to the care of the parent or guardian. Another safeguard is not to allow anyone who does not have a child check into the area where children are present.

In addition to providing a record of all the children who are in a particular area of the church, check-in/checkout procedures can minimize the following risks:

- a stranger leaving with a child,
- a noncustodial parent leaving with a child,
- a child wandering off or trying to leave on his or her own, and
- an intruder entering the child care/education area.

Supervise With Adequate Staff-to-Child / Youth Ratios

If a worker has too many young people to watch, the worker cannot possibly provide adequate supervision. This situation greatly increases the risk of accidents, injuries, and inappropriate behavior.

For all youth activities, and especially overnight retreats, make sure there are enough adult workers (who have been carefully selected and screened) to provide close supervision. Again, if your church has a question about what is an adequate number of supervisors for an off-site or overnight event, consider contacting the local school district to see how it handles supervision needs in similar situations; then follow that procedure. In this way, the church is protecting both the children under its care and the organization itself from claims of negligent supervision.

When it comes to younger children, proper staff-to-child ratios are extremely important as well. In fact, if your church operates a child care service or nursery, be sure to check local and state requirements for mandatory staff-to-child ratios. In general, however, we recommend the following minimum ratios and suggest that they be included in your church's Child and Youth Protection Policy. Whenever possible, consider increasing the number of adult supervisors beyond these levels.

Children's Ages	Adult-to-Child Ratios
2 weeks to 2 years	1:4
2 years	1:6
3 years	1:8
4 years	1:12
5 years and up	1:15

Establish Restroom Procedures

To protect children from abuse and staff members from the appearance of inappropriate behavior, restroom procedures for children should be established by the church and included in the Child and Youth Protection Policy.

We recommend that children who are 5 years old and younger use a classroom bathroom if one is available. If not, workers should escort a group of children to a hallway bathroom. When the group arrives at the bathroom, the workers should check it to make sure the room is empty, and then allow the children inside. The workers should remain outside of the bathroom door and escort all the children back to the room when everyone is finished. If a child is taking longer than seems necessary, workers should open the bathroom door and call the child's name. If the child requires assistance, the workers should prop open the bathroom door and leave the stall door open as they assist the child. A worker should never take a child to the bathroom alone.

For children above the age of 5, at least one (preferably two) adult male should take the boys to the restroom, and at least one (preferably two) adult female should take girls. The worker(s) should check the bathroom first to make sure that it's empty; then the children can be allowed inside. The worker(s) should then remain outside the bathroom door and escort the children back to the classroom.

To protect everyone, a worker should never be alone with a child in a bathroom with a door closed and never in a closed bathroom stall with a child. Parents should be encouraged to have their children visit the bathroom prior to each class.

Teenage Workers

One question that arises frequently is whether, and under what circumstances, teenage workers can assist in caring for younger children at the church. Bear in mind the statistic that the offender in 20 percent of church sexual abuse cases is another minor. But we're not just concerned about sexual abuse here. Given their limited experience and still-developing practical skills, teenage workers are subject to lapses in judgment that can have harmful consequences for the children under their care.

For example, during church choir practice, the 4-year-old daughter of a choir member was left in the care of two girls, ages 14 and 12, without adult supervision. The 4-year-old stood in a wagon while being pulled by one of the girls watching her. The child fell out of the wagon and landed on her head, suffering a traumatic brain injury that required emergency surgery.

Even so, there is certainly a place for teenage workers assisting with younger children at the church, provided safeguards such as the following are in place:

1. Establish a minimum age, such as 14, for volunteer workers.
2. Consider requiring that workers under 18 go through specific training such as the Red Cross baby-sitting safety course.
3. Screen young workers as you would adult workers. The only exception here is that criminal background checks of juveniles are of limited utility. If a background check cannot be run, be extra vigilant about checking references (such as baby-sitting customers or charities) where the minor has volunteered with children in the past.
4. Require that at least one adult provide supervision. Underage workers should never be left alone with children from the church.

Train Your Staff

We mentioned the need to provide employees and volunteers with a copy of the Child and Youth Protection Policy and require them to read it and follow the procedures. While this is an excellent first step in any program, your church can create a much safer environment for children and youth if the staff participates in additional ongoing training, particularly for prevention of child sexual abuse.

Many churches now require all staff and volunteers who will be working with children and youth to complete an initial training course on sexual misconduct prevention. Such a course not only reinforces the church's commitment to protecting youngsters and a no-tolerance policy for abuse, but it also provides the staff with a much greater understanding of the problem, risks involved, warning signs, and how to properly handle a variety of situations.

Today, a number of excellent training programs are available that can be purchased for a nominal fee. Online training to help volunteers prevent sexual abuse at church is available at www.safechurch.com.

Church Volunteer Central

Created by Group Publishing, Church Volunteer Central (CVC) at www .churchvolunteercentral.com is a dynamic, online resource that offers tools, programs, materials, and other information to recruit, train, affirm, and equip church volunteers to be effective.

How to Respond to an Allegation of Sexual Misconduct

We sincerely hope your church will never hear these words: "I think a guy who works here molested my child." But if an allegation of sexual misconduct is made by a parent, guardian, or church worker, it is absolutely critical to know how to respond. Without the proper response, the situation can go from bad to worse. There can even be criminal penalties if a pastor is a "mandatory reporter" under your state's child abuse reporting law and fails to report the abuse to authorities.

If an incident of abuse is suspected or alleged to have occurred at the church or during a church-sponsored event or activity, the church's pre-established general procedures should be used. Suggestions for such are explained in greater detail in the "Response Procedures for Sexual Misconduct Allegations," available in the *SafeChurch Resource Packet* (free for download at www.safechurch.com). But in short, all responses should be to take any allegation seriously, to report it immediately to relevant church authorities, and to comply with all state laws (especially pertaining to the reporting of allegations to legal authorities), which should result in an investigation.

Nursery and Toddler Area Safety

Church-operated nurseries and toddler areas can be convenient programs for parents and enriching for children. However, churches that have nurseries and toddler areas on-site must be fully aware of the risks associated with caring for very young children. A variety of steps must be taken to minimize those risks with proper safety and security measures. Ultimately, the church must assume full responsibility for the well-being of every child entrusted to the organization.

There are numerous safety, security, and health issues to consider if your church operates a nursery, toddler area, or similar program. As described in the previous sections, all procedures for hiring, selecting, and screening workers should be followed for the nursery/toddler area, as well as supervision guidelines and sign-in/sign-out procedures for the children. We recommend the following additional safeguards and considerations:

Inspect and Safeguard the Area

Any area in the church that is used for a nursery or toddler care should be inspected on a weekly basis to identify hazards. Modifications to the area may also be necessary so it provides children with the safest and most secure environment possible. For instance, windows should be installed on doors and/or walls wherever appropriate to provide clear views of all child care rooms. Any exterior or closet doors should be kept locked. Windows should be kept securely locked. Protective covers should be installed on electrical outlets, and any hazards should be removed or repaired.

The "Nursery and Toddler Area Safety Checklist" is available in the *SafeChurch Resource Packet* (free for download at www.safechurch.com) and provides a practical tool for weekly inspections.

Supervise workers. Make sure all child care workers are properly supervised by a qualified individual. On a regular basis, but at unannounced times, a supervisor should tour the child care areas to see how everything is going. It's always best if workers know that a supervisor may stop by at any time of the day.

Consider video security cameras. Because of the many recent advances in technology, the use of security cameras in child care facilities is a fast-growing trend. The cost of these cameras has become surprisingly affordable, and there are many types to choose from, including webcam services that allow parents to view their children via the Internet. According to the proponents of security cameras, the cameras are an effective deterrent to abuse, they may scare perpetrators away, and they keep a constant eye on the actions of workers and children.

Playground Safety

Head injuries—While playing on a church's playground equipment, a 5-year-old boy fell off a 4-foot platform and landed headfirst on the ground. When he stood up, there was blood trickling from his ear, and surgery was later performed to remove pressure from the boy's brain. His parents filed a lawsuit against the church claiming there was not enough cushioning material below the playground equipment. The church said it had ordered additional sand for the playground three weeks earlier, but the sand did not arrive until three days after the accident. The church had no records to prove when the sand order had been placed.

Compound fractures—New playground equipment was installed at a church, and mulch was going to be added to the area at a later time by church workers. Before the mulch was put down, children were allowed to play on the equipment, and a 7-year-old girl fell from the monkey bars, which were 7 feet, 3 inches high. Upon landing on the hard ground below, the girl sustained a compound fracture of the arm and had a broken bone protruding from her skin. The girl's parents filed a lawsuit against the church. Although the church had placed caution tape up to keep children out of the woods nearby, there was no caution tape placed on the new playground equipment. The lawsuit was eventually settled for $150,000.

Playground Injury Statistics

- More than 200,000 children are treated in emergency rooms each year for playground-related injuries.
- Nearly 80 percent of playground injuries involve falls, and over half of the time a child's head and/or face is hurt.
- Most injuries are preventable with proper supervision and safer playground surfaces, equipment, and design.

If you have a playground at your church or are considering building one, it can be another high-risk area where children can easily be hurt or seriously injured. To make sure your playground is as safe as it can be, it is critical to follow some basic guidelines.

Basic Playground Practices

Install proper surfaces. This is one of the most important ways to prevent or minimize injuries when children fall on playgrounds. If the surface under playground equipment is both soft and thick enough, it can help absorb the shock of a child's fall. Acceptable surfaces include loosely filled materials like wood chips, mulch, sand, pea gravel, or shredded rubber. Surfacing mats made of safety-tested rubber or rubberlike materials may also be used. Concrete, asphalt, and blacktop are unsafe and unacceptable. Grass, soil, and packed-earth surfaces are unsafe as well.

The proper depth (thickness) of safe surface material depends on the height of playground equipment. But generally, 12 inches of depth should be used for equipment up to 8 feet high. The surface material must not be packed down because packing will lessen any cushioning effect. Surface materials should also cover appropriate-sized "fall zones" (the areas surrounding any equipment where children could possibly fall). For instance, surfacing for climbing equipment and slides should extend a minimum of 6 feet in every direction. (Adding 4 feet to the height of the slide gives a good estimate of how much surfacing should extend beyond the exit slope of the slide). And swings need surfacing in front and back, two times the height of the swing set, and 6 feet on either side of the swing set support beams.

Install fencing. Consider having your playground enclosed with a fence or a natural barrier such as a hedge. The fence or barrier should be at least 4 feet high and no more than 3 inches off the ground. The fence or barrier serves a couple of purposes: It encloses the playground to prevent children from wandering away, and it also provides a barrier to keep unauthorized persons from easily accessing the playground and the children playing there without being noticed.

Provide adult supervision. A sufficient number of adults should always be on hand to supervise children when the playground is in use. Young children (and some older kids) often cannot judge distances accurately or foresee dangerous situations. For example, children should not wear hoods, attached mittens, or other clothing with strings on the playground because of the risk of strangulation if the strings were to get caught on playground equipment.

For these reasons and more, adult supervisors are extremely important and can help prevent injuries by making sure kids don't act unsafely or use equipment improperly. If an injury does occur, an adult supervisor will be able to act quickly to offer first aid or other assistance. In addition, adult supervisors should teach children how to play safely on the equipment and establish rules that must be followed, such as no pushing or playing Tag on the equipment, only one person at a time on the slide, and no sliding headfirst.

For a detailed list of key playground safety measures, refer to and apply the "Playground Safety Factors" in the *SafeChurch Resource Packet* (free for download at www.safechurch.com).

Recreational Activity Safety

Remember the days when you were a free-spirited youth? When you were involved in a recreational or athletic activity, did you worry about getting hurt? Chances are, safety was the last thing on your mind. Having fun was your only concern.

Young people have the same carefree attitude today. Whenever they're with a group of their peers and caught up in the action, they have little if any fear and can easily get hurt—especially during recreational activities and sports. As you can imagine, if the proper precautions are not taken for many activities, a serious injury could result, causing tremendous sorrow for everyone involved. What's more, the incident can become much worse if a liability lawsuit is filed against your church.

Here are just two horror stories to illustrate the potential for accidents:

Deadly Test of Strength—A large group of senior high school students was attending a "rush weekend" event at a Christian camp. During an organized test-of-strength activity, a rope was tied to a 1970 Ford bus, and eight or nine youths were pulling the bus forward. As a volunteer sat in the driver's seat of the bus with the engine running, the boy who was closest to the front of the bus somehow fell and the bus ran over him. He died from his injuries.

Fatal Boating Accident—During a youth group trip to a lake, the church pastor was using his own boat to pull kids on a ski tube in the water. When a 17-year-old boy was taking his turn, he fell off the ski tube, and the pastor circled the boat around. The boy indicated he wanted to go for another ride, but then attempted to climb into the boat without warning. The boat's propeller struck the boy's leg and severed an artery. He was airlifted to a hospital but never regained consciousness. He died from loss of blood.

Churches Are Offering a Wider Variety of Activities

As churches continue to expand their ministries and reach out to more people in the community, many are offering an increasing variety of recreational opportunities on their campuses. Gymnasiums, playgrounds, outdoor basketball courts, and softball and soccer fields are some of the most common. But skateboard parks, climbing walls, inflatable rides, and swimming pools are gaining in popularity as well.

While each type of activity calls for its own specific set of safeguards, here are general policies and procedures that churches can implement to enhance safety and reduce the risks:

- Require that all activities be preapproved by a specified group of church leaders, such as your Church Safety and Security Team.
- Establish written guidelines for youth activities, and carefully monitor and supervise all events.
- Implement an application and acceptance process for selecting staff and volunteers who will work with youth and children during activities. This should include criminal background checks.

- Train staff and volunteers on safe transportation of youth, and develop a written transportation policy including driver qualification requirements. (See Chapter 9 for more details.)
- Require an appropriate ratio of adults to youth at each event. Two or more adults should always be present.
- Assess risks of the activity and inform leaders about possible hazards prior to each event. Train leaders to discontinue the activity if safety considerations dictate (for example, if lightning approaches during an outdoor activity).
- Require that consent and emergency medical forms be signed by parents before their children are allowed to participate.
- Keep records of current phone numbers to contact parents in case of emergencies.
- Inform parents in writing about all activities.
- Train and certify leaders in courses such as first aid and CPR.
- Have leaders carry cell phones during all events and activities.

Adult Supervision Is Key

If young people are allowed to participate in a recreational activity with little or no supervision, it is an invitation to disaster. Horseplay and disregard for safety rules are common causes of injuries among adolescents. This is why it's essential to always have an adequate number of adults on hand to supervise all recreational activities. At a minimum, two unrelated adults should supervise every group. If the group is larger, there should be an appropriate adult-to-youth ratio to provide adequate supervision.

In the event of injury, at least two adult supervisors will be needed to help ensure that the appropriate actions are taken immediately. It will take at least one adult to provide first aid and call for help while the other adult supervises the remainder of the group. Also, it's usually best not to rely on teenage supervisors because they may lack the necessary judgment in emergency situations.

First-Aid Training and Supplies

No matter what type of recreational activity is taking place, make sure the church and supervisors are well prepared to administer first aid if needed.

- There should be at least one adult supervisor present who has received formal first-aid training that includes certification in CPR.

- A well-stocked first-aid kit should be kept on hand and easily accessible to supervisors.
- Supervisors should always carry cell phones or have easy access to a telephone in case they need to call 911 in an emergency situation.
- For larger groups or events such as a basketball or softball tournament, recruit a certified nurse, emergency medical technician (EMT), or doctor from the congregation to be on-site.

Documentation for Participation

No one enjoys filling out forms, but to enhance the safety of participants and reduce risks for the church, it's wise to require the following forms for all youngsters who will be participating in an activity. Examples of these forms are available in the *SafeChurch Resource Packet* (free for download at www.safechurch.com).

- "Parent or Guardian of a Minor Consent and Hold Harmless"
- "Parent or Guardian Consent to Treat a Minor"

Once completed, these forms should be kept on file at the church in a central location where supervisors can access them easily in case of an emergency. The consent forms will help ensure that parents and guardians are aware of the type of activity their children will be engaging in and the potential risks involved. They can also serve as legal documents, if necessary. As two more safeguards, consider asking participants to complete a health history form and to provide contact information in case an emergency should arise.

"Youth and Child Accident/Incident Report"—If a young person is injured during a recreational activity, a supervisor should be required to fill out an accident/ incident report that describes details such as the time and location of the accident, how it occurred, and the type of first aid or professional medical assistance that was provided. See the *SafeChurch Resource Packet* (free for download at www .safechurch.com) for an example.

Get legal and insurance advice. Finally, we strongly encourage churches to consult with both an attorney and a professional insurance agent about the liabilities associated with a recreational activity and to determine whether special insurance coverage is needed. In some cases, a church's standard liability insurance protection may not cover certain high-risk activities.

Youth Trips and Overnight Retreats

Partly because of a lack of screening and criminal background checks, a 20-year-old man who had a previous rape conviction was allowed to work as a church camp counselor. He eventually began a sexual relationship with a 14-year-old girl attending the camp. Although the man's actions with the girl resulted in a criminal conviction, the incident had a devastating impact on the church's ministry and ended up in an insurance claim that cost more than $1 million.

We cannot overemphasize the number of risks that are involved when churches sponsor youth trips, overnight retreats, and other off-site events. From the moment young people climb into vehicles to the time they return, a host of problems can occur, including traffic accidents, sexual misconduct of staff and/or participants, injuries during activities, and other nightmare scenarios. The church can also be held legally liable for any unfortunate incidents that take place during the event.

When you consider the number of risks involved, youth trips and overnight retreats require careful planning, increased adult supervision, and a variety of other important safeguards and procedures. Many of the steps have been discussed in previous sections, but to assist your church in preparing for a youth trip or overnight retreat, the "Youth Trip and Overnight Retreat Checklist" is a valuable guide (available in the *SafeChurch Resource Packet,* which is free for download at www.safechurch.com).

Churches are advised (as part of this checklist) to be especially diligent about supervising high-risk activities such as youth trips and overnight retreats. When risks increase, supervision should also increase.

Computer and Internet Safety for Youth

Many people have seen TV news reports about how sexual predators use the Internet and online chat rooms to find their victims. In several sting operations broadcast by TV news magazines, adults posing as teenagers in chat rooms had conversations with men who wanted to meet the teenagers for sexual encounters. When the men arrived to meet their underage "victims" in person, they were confronted by a reporter, a TV camera, and the police. These reports illustrate just how dangerous the Internet can be for young people who are not careful about who they are communicating with online.

If your church has computers that young people can use for Internet access, or if you allow individuals to bring their own computers to church and access the Internet, special safety precautions, rules, and policies should be established for computer use.

In addition to being exposed to the danger of meeting sexual predators online, children and youth could also be exposed to pornographic images, videos, and frightening messages.

Adhere to the following principles to safeguard children and youth during computer and Internet use:

- Adults should supervise teenagers when they are using computers at the church.
- Churches should be very cautious about hosting chat rooms, blogs, discussion groups, or other online forums involving the church's youth. If such forums are considered, guidelines should be established concerning appropriate online conduct and sharing of personal information and photographs. Parental consent for each child's involvement is recommended. Such forums should be monitored by a designated church leader.
- It's also wise to consider providing education to youth group members about the dangers of posting photos or personal profiles on social websites and/or communicating with unknown persons online.
- Install filters and other software on church computers to prevent children and youth from accessing inappropriate websites or receiving pornographic images. And on a regular basis, have an adult check the online history of computers being used at the church. This will provide a record of which websites are being visited by the users.

Wrap a Security Blanket Around Your Kids

No, you cannot hope to protect children and youth from every danger they may encounter 24 hours a day. But at least when young people are at your facilities or in the church's care, your organization can take a wide variety of steps to ensure children and youth are as safe and secure as possible.

By investing some time, energy, and resources to develop a comprehensive Child and Youth Protection Policy that everyone is required to follow, your church may save a child's life, prevent a case of sexual misconduct, or avoid any number of other heartbreaking situations. Safeguarding our precious children is one of the most important and rewarding aspects of any risk management program.

Chapter 9

Transportation Safety

One Passenger Killed, 11 Injured When Church Van Rolls Over

One large, Midwestern church knows all too well about the dangers of transporting church members.

Over the years, the church had rented many 15-passenger vans for mission trips to Mexico. The journeys to and from Mexico had always gone smoothly and without incident until 2000, when a tragic accident occurred.

While 12 members were traveling on an interstate in a nearly new 15-passenger van, the volunteer driver began to change lanes. When she realized there was another vehicle in the van's blind spot, she swerved back into her lane and lost control of the vehicle. It rolled onto the median, crashing into a guardrail. All 12 occupants were wearing their seat belts, but everyone sustained serious injuries, some critical. One passenger, a 15-year-old girl, was killed in the crash. Because of the devastating loss, the mission trip was canceled and the more than 100 participants returned home.

"That accident was heartbreaking for the entire church and community," an administrator at the church recalled. "From that point on, we stopped using 15-passenger vans—period. Now, anytime we're going on a trip of any length, we charter buses for the participants. Even though it's more expensive, the buses are a much safer way to travel."

As the administrator pointed out, along with the inherent risks of 15-passenger vans, which have been publicized in the media, churches face the additional risk of many volunteer drivers having little or no experience operating such vehicles. "One of the big problems is, 15-passenger vans do not require a CDL (commercial driver's license), and the people who drive them are usually not familiar with the handling characteristics of the vans," he said. "That makes traveling in them even more dangerous."

In addition to banning the use of 15-passenger vans for church-related trips and leasing charter buses instead, the church also now utilizes shuttle buses for its local transportation needs. "The shuttles we use require CDLs to operate, and again, they are much safer than 15-passenger vans."

Accident in a Privately Owned Car

Because there was a large turnout for a church youth retreat, one of the younger volunteer teachers was asked to drive three members to the event. Although drivers for the church were supposed to have valid licenses and proper auto insurance, the youth teacher was using his father's automobile, which had no insurance coverage because the policy had lapsed. The car was also missing its front passenger seat and had only two seat belts for the occupants in back. When the teacher and his three passengers departed for the event and entered the freeway at a high rate of speed, the vehicle went out of control, struck a traffic light pole, and rolled over. Luckily, no one was killed, but everyone in the car sustained serious injuries, requiring hospitalization, long-term care, and rehabilitation. As a result of the accident, the cost to settle claims for the injured passengers reached $1 million.

Volunteer Leader Flips SUV

At another church, volunteer leaders were providing transportation to a youth group event. While one of the leaders was driving her SUV to carry seven passengers, she allowed her vehicle to drift off the roadway. She struck a milepost marker, swerved back into the lane of travel, and then lost control, causing the vehicle to flip over two times. All of the occupants were injured in the accident, including a 14-year-old girl, who was thrown approximately 50 feet from the vehicle. She suffered a fractured spine, fractured wrist, and dislocated shoulder and required emergency surgery. To settle the injury claims, the driver's personal insurance company paid their policy limit of $250,000, and an additional $500,000 was paid by the church and its insurance company.

Dangers of the Road

Needless to say, when serious accidents like these occur, they shatter the lives of the victims, their families, and friends. Every member of the church is devastated by the loss, and it takes years for a ministry to heal. And those who were partially responsible for the accident may suffer a lifetime of guilt. Let's all pray that your church never experiences such pain.

U.S. Traffic Accident Statistics in 2006

- 42,642 people were killed in motor vehicle crashes. 30,521 of the people killed were occupants of passenger vehicles.
- 2.5 million people were injured in motor vehicle crashes. 2.3 million were occupants of passenger vehicles.
- Among the vehicle occupants who were killed, 17,800 were riding in passenger cars, and 12,721 were in light trucks and vans.
- 10,698 people were killed in rollover crashes.
- More than half (55 percent) of the people who were killed as occupants in passenger vehicles were not wearing seat belts.

SOURCE: *2006 Annual Assessment of Motor Vehicle Crashes,* published September 2007 by the National Highway Traffic Safety Association's (NHTSA) National Center for Statistics and Analysis

If you drove a vehicle to church this week, hopefully you wore a seat belt, traveled cautiously, and arrived without any trouble. But as you were driving, did it ever cross your mind just how dangerous it is to travel on the road?

In addition to the statistics and horror stories presented in this chapter's introduction, here are two more sobering thoughts: According to the National Safety Council, the lifetime odds of dying in some type of motor vehicle accident are approximately 1 in 84. And the odds of being injured in a vehicle accident are 1 in 1.6, which is greater than a 50 percent chance.

Granted, despite the dangers of driving or riding in a vehicle, it would be extremely difficult for most people—as well as most churches—to avoid transportation risks entirely. Furthermore, as ministries continue to expand in scope and are involved in off-campus activities, such as retreats and mission trips, churches' need for transportation continues to grow.

Since nearly every church utilizes vehicles in one way or another, as a leader of your organization or member of the Church Safety and Security (CSS) Team, it is imperative to recognize that one of the most devastating risks your church faces is the operation of motor vehicles for church-related events and business. The more often transportation is used, the greater this risk becomes.

You know how easily a motor vehicle crash can occur. And if the accident is serious, your church can be held legally liable for any damages, injuries, or deaths that occur during church-related transportation. Plus, your church can be held accountable whether it owns, leases, rents, or borrows the vehicle, or has volunteers and staff members who use their own personal vehicles for church-sponsored transportation. Even the drivers who are involved in serious accidents can be held legally liable or face criminal charges. In most cases, it is the driver's legal responsibility to make sure passengers comply with seat belt laws and child-restraint laws. If an accident occurs, the driver can be charged in both civil and criminal courts.

Aside from those risks, the safety of your members, volunteers, and staff is, of course, the number one reason to be concerned about the use of vehicles. Therefore, to help keep everyone safe, while also reducing the church's exposure to potential accidents, transportation safety should be another top priority in your church's risk management efforts.

As with many risks your church needs to address, one of the best ways to get started with a transportation safety program is by looking at the big picture and identifying key areas of need. To accomplish this initial goal, please ask your church leaders and CSS Team to complete the "Transportation Safety Survey" in the *SafeChurch Resource Packet* (free for download at www.safechurch.com).

Reduce the Dangers

Realistically, not every vehicle accident can be prevented. However, a large number of accidents are caused by situations and factors that could have been avoided, such as poor maintenance, unsafe equipment, improper selection of drivers, driver or passenger error, driver fatigue, or improper selection or use of a vehicle. By being proactive and addressing the transportation issues that your church *can* control, you will greatly reduce the chances of experiencing an accident or minimize its severity. For instance, an accident may damage a vehicle, but by simply requiring all passengers to wear their seat belts on every trip, a life could be saved.

Form a Transportation Team

Transportation safety is such an important issue that it requires one or more individuals at your church to spearhead the effort and oversee implementation. To achieve this objective, we urge churches to form a Transportation Team or appoint a transportation director and assistant. At some smaller churches, a single director and assistant may be sufficient. But if the church owns vehicles or uses vehicles on a fairly frequent basis, a Transportation Team is highly recommended.

The Transportation Team can be made up of members of the Church Safety and Security Team if they have time and can take on this additional responsibility. However, it may be best to recruit a small group of people who can serve on the Transportation Team and make it their primary focus. The team can consist of one or more staff members, drivers, maintenance workers, and parents, or whatever group of people is passionate about this issue. Members of the team can be rotated in and out of the group as needed, but try to keep one or more members with experience on the team at all times so they can share their knowledge with incoming team members.

One of the first goals of the Transportation Team is to develop a written transportation policy. (Policy recommendations and easy-to-use forms will be described in the upcoming sections.) Once the written policy has been created, the team should obtain whatever approval is needed by your church's governance structure. The team should continue to meet quarterly to ensure the policy is being followed, drivers are being monitored, vehicles remain in compliance, and maintenance is being performed and documented as scheduled.

Developing a Transportation Policy

The more often your church transports members or has staff members who drive for church business, the greater the chances of experiencing an accident. Even though most of your church's employees and volunteers are probably responsible drivers, all it takes is one mistake, a mechanical failure, faulty equipment, or a lapse in judgment for an accident to occur. A fender bender might be no big deal, but if passengers are seriously injured or killed in the accident, it will have a devastating impact on the ministry. To help avoid such a tragedy and minimize risks, a transportation policy is essential. The policy will establish consistent procedures and guidelines aimed at avoiding unnecessary risks, identifying mechanical problems, and making everyone aware of his or her responsibilities.

What's more, if your church should ever experience a serious accident, the transportation policy and written records can help demonstrate that the church was not negligent. If proper records are kept as required in the policy, the church will have documentation of the steps that were taken to prevent an accident.

We've provided a variety of transportation-related forms and templates in downloadable formats in the *SafeChurch Resource Packet* (free for download at www.safechurch.com). Using them will make the development of a transportation policy much easier. Here are the forms you will find:

- "Transportation Worker Application Form"
- "Vehicle Self-Inspection Report and Instructions"
- "Accident/Incident Report"

The transportation policy that your church creates should, of course, be tailored to the needs of your organization, the types of vehicles used, drivers, and other factors. Once created, it should be reviewed and approved by church leaders, the CSS Team, as well as an attorney, if possible. In general, a transportation policy should include the following elements:

Driver Selection Procedures

You've probably seen this situation occur: Just prior to an off-site church event, a group of participants, including staff, parents, and teenagers, meet at the church. Depending on how many people show up and who can drive, passengers are divided into small groups to ride in the cars, minivans, and SUVs that are available and have room. Several teenagers may want to drive their own cars and take a few friends. All climb in their vehicles and caravan to the event.

While such informal travel arrangements may work out just fine, this can be an extremely risky way to travel to a church event. For instance, what if a teen driver becomes distracted by his cell phone and gets in an accident? Or maybe one of the parents has poor eyesight or a history of accidents? Caravanning can also be unsafe because one vehicle may follow another too closely. The list of risks goes on and on.

It's also common for churches to allow just about anyone with a license to drive a vehicle owned by the church.

Instead of taking these unnecessary risks and hoping that drivers are qualified, churches should carefully select all drivers prior to transporting members. Address the following procedures for driver selection in your church's transportation policy:

Establish age requirements. Studies show that accident rates are the highest for drivers under 25 years of age and over 70. That's why it's wise to allow only people who are between 25 and 70 to drive others to and from church events.

Require drivers to complete application forms. Before drivers are allowed to drive for the church, require them to complete a "Transportation Worker Application Form." (Please see the *SafeChurch Resource Packet,* free for download at www .safechurch.com, for an example.) This form will establish a documented process for selecting qualified and eligible drivers for church-related events. In addition to gathering general information such as name, address, age, and phone numbers, the application should also request the following:

- driver's license number and information
- driver training/experience
- traffic violation history
- any history of child abuse or criminal convictions
- insurance information
- medical or visual conditions that might affect driving abilities
- personal automobile information (if the vehicle will be used in church transportation)
- employment history
- education
- previous church affiliations
- references
- permission for the church to conduct a background check and investigate motor vehicle records, past employment, and so on

Check motor vehicle and criminal records. Far too many church vehicle accidents involve drivers with unknown histories of traffic violations or accidents, criminal records, and substance abuse. Therefore, before allowing anyone to operate a vehicle for your church, be sure to conduct a criminal and motor vehicle records check on each potential driver. Obtain permission from the driver for this screening during the driver application process. By requiring this important step in your transportation policy, your church will have the opportunity to screen and disqualify any driver who has had problems in the past and poses an unnecessary risk.

In addition, consider checking your drivers' motor vehicle records on an ongoing basis, such as once a year. In this way, your church will remain updated on the driving records of its drivers.

Require proper insurance. It is imperative that all vehicles have the proper levels of insurance coverage. If your church owns one or more vehicles, a business auto policy should be purchased, and an umbrella policy for $1 million or more is strongly recommended. If staff and volunteers are driving their own cars for the church, require that they provide proof of their insurance. While requirements for passenger vehicle insurance coverage vary from state to state, a minimum of $100,000 to $300,000 is recommended. If the church rents vehicles or allows drivers to use their personal vehicles to provide church-sponsored transportation, the church should secure "non-owned and hired" automobile liability coverage. This is separate coverage from the business auto policy and is important to protect the church from liability in the event the non-owned vehicle is not sufficiently insured. Finally, if the church is hiring a driver to operate a bus or van, the driver or company offering the service should be required to present proof of insurance and have the church added as an additional insured on that party's policy.

Select Vehicles Carefully

As part of your transportation policy, determine procedures for selecting vehicles for church use. For instance, if the church will be using a non-owned vehicle (privately owned by an employee or volunteer), the vehicle should be inspected by a member of the Transportation Team to ensure it is in safe operating condition. Requirements should include seat belts for all occupants, safe brakes, good tires, working windshield wipers, window cleaner, proper mirrors, defroster, first-aid kit, and adequate insurance. This selection-inspection process should also be performed if the church is renting or borrowing a vehicle.

If your church is considering buying or leasing a vehicle, predetermined requirements within your transportation policy can help ensure that the safest vehicles are selected. We recommend the following:

- Consider alternatives to 15-passenger vans. The National Highway Traffic Safety Administration (NHTSA) has issued several national warnings to users of 15-passenger vans that the vans have an increased risk of rollover crashes under certain conditions. (See the "15-Passenger Van Risks and Safety Precautions" section in this chapter for more details.)
- Recommend or require the use of multifunction school activity buses, which offer superior levels of safety. (See the description at the end of this chapter.)
- Evaluate other vehicle options such as minivans and cars with adequate safety features. Quality minivans and cars are safer than 15-passenger vans.

Provide Driver Training

Once drivers have been selected and meet all necessary criteria, the church can greatly enhance transportation safety by requiring drivers to complete one or more training courses. Driver training is especially important for the operation of buses and vans. Many driver training programs are available online to assist with training. For instance, a 15-passenger van driver training course can be accessed at the SafeChurch website at www.safechurch.com. We recommend that drivers be trained in the following areas:

- general instruction on safe operation of all vehicles to be driven;
- defensive driving;
- special training for operators of 15-passenger vans, which pose higher risks of rollover crashes;
- proper passenger loading and unloading procedures; and
- instruction on route planning, safety equipment, emergency response procedures, and accident-report filing.

All training should be documented and kept on file.

Inspect and Maintain Vehicles Regularly

Many transportation accidents are caused by unsafe vehicles and poorly maintained equipment, such as worn or improperly inflated tires, faulty brake systems, and windshield wipers that do not work. But with frequent inspections and regular maintenance, a wide variety of equipment problems can be identified and corrected before they become dangerous.

For vehicles that are rented or privately owned by staff and volunteers who will be driving for the church, safety inspections of the vehicles should be required as part of the selection process. For all church-owned and leased vehicles, the following specific requirements for ongoing inspections and maintenance should be established:

- Identify who is responsible for overseeing inspections and maintenance of vehicles including state requirements such as safety inspections, emissions testing, and vehicle registration renewals.
- Determine how often each vehicle should be professionally serviced. (Semiannual inspections and service with a qualified mechanic are recommended.)
- Require the completion of a pre- and post-trip inspection checklist.
- Document inspections and maintenance records.

For your own needs, please refer to and reproduce the "Vehicle Self-Inspection Report and Instructions" in the *SafeChurch Resource Packet* (free for download at www.safechurch.com).

Establish Safety Rules for Passengers and Drivers

When children and teenagers are traveling to or from a church event, safety concerns are the last things on their minds. For instance, if youngsters are not reminded to wear seat belts, they can easily forget to fasten them or think it's "uncool." Or several teenagers on a bus may start dancing to music while driving down the road. These are just a few of the reasons safety rules need to be established, communicated to everyone, and closely followed. (See the box below for an example of rules for the road.)

Rules for drivers are equally important and should be defined in the transportation policy as well. This will help stress the importance of their role; their responsibility for safety; and their need to adhere to all traffic laws, speed limits, and other motor vehicle requirements. If a passenger observes any misconduct or dangerous behavior by a driver, the incident should be reported to the Transportation Team immediately.

Rules for the Road

Prior to any church-related trip, the following safety rules should be communicated to all participants, whether they're traveling in church-owned or private vehicles. The organizer and/or driver for the trip should ensure that all participants read, understand, and sign the following rules:

- Seat belts must be worn at all times.
- No hazardous, disruptive activity or noise will be permitted while the vehicle is moving. All passengers must follow the driver's requests.
- All objects must be kept inside the vehicle.
- All windows must be kept clear of objects that may disrupt the driver's view.
- In case of an accident or emergency, stop and do not exit the vehicle unless instructed to do so by the driver. Always exit on the sidewalk (non-traffic) side of the vehicle and never on the traffic side.
- Violation of these rules may result in canceling the trip for the entire group or the removal of a participant from the trip.
- The safety of others and myself are the top priorities on this trip.

I have read, understand, and will comply with these rules during the entire trip.

Name _____

Date _____

Require Safety and Survival Equipment in Vehicles

In the event of an accident, emergency, or other problem encountered on the road, the proper safety equipment can help minimize dangers, treat injuries, or prevent the situation from becoming worse. If your church is transporting members on an extended trip, include these items in a safety and survival kit:

- accident reporting forms
- communication devices for use between vehicles (cellular/mobile telephone or two-way radio, for example)
- blankets
- bottled water
- duct tape
- emergency phone numbers (for example, road service, church, pastor)
- fire extinguisher (dry chemical)
- first-aid kit
- flashlight and batteries
- insurance information
- jumper cables
- maps
- warning reflectors
- paper towels and toilet tissue
- radio with fresh batteries
- rags and towels

Create Accident Response and Reporting Procedures

Finally, it's wise for the church to establish accident response and reporting procedures for drivers to follow if an accident does occur. These will help the driver act in the most effective manner and record vital information about the accident and individuals involved. This involves filing an "Accident/Incident Report," which includes a "Preliminary Traffic Accident Report." This two-part form is available in the *SafeChurch Resource Packet* (free for download at www .safechurch.com).

15-Passenger Van Risks and Safety Precautions

Because of their size and relatively affordable cost, 15-passenger vans became extremely popular for church transportation. However, beginning in 2001, numerous warnings were issued and publicized in the media about the high risks of rollover crashes and injuries from side impacts in 15-passenger vans.

According to the most recent statistics when this book was published, rollover accidents involving 15-passenger vans killed 1,062 passengers or drivers and seriously injured an additional 1,867 van occupants from 1982 to 2006.

When combined with other risk factors, such as the lack of seat belt use, poor driver selection, and improper maintenance, the potential for fatal and debilitating injuries in van accidents continues to be a very serious concern.

If your church owns or utilizes one or more 15-passenger vans—especially older models—it is extremely important to recognize the risks of operating such vehicles and to take appropriate steps to eliminate or minimize the dangers.

NHTSA Warnings

In 2001, the National Highway Traffic Safety Administration issued its first national warning to drivers of 15-passenger vans that the vehicles posed an increased risk of rollover crashes under certain conditions.

According to the 2001 NHTSA research study, when 15-passenger vans are fully loaded, the center of gravity shifts rearward and upward, increasing the likelihood of a rollover occurring. This shift also increases the potential for loss of control in panic maneuvers. Additionally, NHTSA said the design of 15-passenger vans is not conducive to handling side impacts, and many injuries and deaths attributed to the vans are the result of passenger ejection, either due to lack of seat belt availability or use.

The introductory story in this chapter illustrates just how dangerous a van accident can be.

Van Rollover Risks

Rollover risks rise dramatically as the number of van occupants increases. With 10 or more occupants, the rollover rate is nearly three times that of vans that are lightly loaded. With more than 15 occupants, the risk of a rollover is almost six times greater than if the van had only five occupants.

SOURCE: 2001 NHTSA research study

NHTSA repeated its 15-passenger van warning in 2002, again in 2004, and then announced additional research in 2005 that reinforced its existing concerns about 15-passenger vans.

In the 2005 research report, which focused on improper tire maintenance on 15-passenger vans, NHTSA found that 74 percent of all 15-passenger vans had significantly over- or underinflated tires by 25 percent or more. By contrast, 39 percent of passenger cars were found with improperly inflated tires. NHTSA's research indicated that improperly inflated tires can change handling characteristics, increasing the potential for a rollover crash in 15-passenger vans.

New Stability Systems Introduced by Ford, Chevy, and GM

Fortunately, the auto industry has recognized the need for additional safety features on 15-passenger vans, and manufacturers are now offering a variety of enhanced stability systems on their large vans. When this book went to press, the following systems were being offered:

- In 2004, General Motors (GM) and Chevrolet introduced new stability-enhancement systems for their 15-passenger vans. Chevrolet claims that its StabiliTrak Electronic Stability Control system can improve vehicle stability, particularly on slick surfaces or during emergency maneuvers. When StabiliTrak senses that the vehicle is not responding to steering input, which can lead to loss of lateral traction (sideslip), understeer (plowing), or oversteer (fishtailing), the system automatically adjusts engine torque and/ or brake pressure at individual wheels to help the driver get the vehicle back on track. In addition, GM and Chevy have also added horizontal crash bars in vans to help better handle side impacts.
- In 2006, Ford introduced a new Roll Stability Control (RSC) system along with AdvanceTrac. According to Ford, the Roll Stability Control builds on the three AdvanceTrac chassis control systems already on the vehicle: anti-lock brakes, traction control, and yaw control. Roll Stability Control adds another component: a gyroscopic sensor that helps monitor vehicle-roll motion. If the RSC system detects a potentially unstable situation, the system automatically applies braking pressure to the appropriate wheels. Ford says this helps keep all four wheels safely on the ground and reduces the risk of rollovers.
- Tire pressure-monitoring systems are another new technology that manufacturers are offering on vans for the 2008 model year. With these systems, a warning sounds when tires are 25 percent underinflated.

Precautions Are Still Essential

As you can see, there is some encouraging news about 15-passenger vans as manufacturers add new stability-control enhancements and other safety features.

Realistically, though, it will take several more years of actual on-road use to determine just how effective the new systems are.

Since thousands of older vans are still in use today, it remains essential for churches that own them to take all necessary precautions to keep passengers safe. And even if your church has purchased a new van or has plans to do so, it's equally important to establish policies and procedures to operate the vehicle safely.

Driver Training and Selection

Earlier in this chapter, we described techniques for proper driver selection, including requirements for driver application forms and checking motor vehicle records. Those screening procedures are even more critical if a driver will be operating a van. In addition, once drivers have been selected, they should be required to participate in additional training to operate a van. Earning a commercial driver's license (CDL) is also recommended.

Training for van drivers is essential because of the vehicles' inherent risks and their unique handling characteristics, which are very different from cars'. Obviously, vans are longer, wider, and heavier than cars and therefore stop more slowly. In windy conditions, vans are more difficult to control. More blind spots are present in vans; they have a longer wheel base and a wider turning radius. But most important, because of vans' high center of gravity, they are more susceptible to tipping and rolling over, especially during rapid or panic maneuvers.

At a minimum, van drivers should successfully complete a defensive driving course to operate 15-passenger vans. Minimum requirements for the course should include instruction time, testing with written results, and driver certification.

Internet-based driver training programs are a convenient option to consider for your church's drivers, and there are a variety of nationally recognized programs that meet minimum requirements. For your convenience, an outstanding, online driver training program is available at www.safechurch.com.

Inspect and Maintain Tires Carefully

To help reduce the risk of rollover accidents, NHTSA began and continues to urge all van owners to maintain their tires carefully. This includes making sure tires are properly selected and inflated and the tread is not worn. Van tires should be load range E. If your van does not have load range E tires, consider replacing them immediately. Improper inflation can also cause handling problems as well as catastrophic tire failures, such as blowouts. NHTSA recommends inspecting tires at least once a week for tread wear and proper inflation. Tires should always be kept inflated to the pressure specified by the vehicle's manufacturer, which can be found on the vehicle's door pillar or in the owner's manual. The recommended air pressures for van tires are significantly different from those for passenger automobiles.

Worn tires present a risk of loss of control and blowouts. If the tread of the tire is less than 1/8 inch or the tires appear to have deteriorated, replace them. For added protection, replace tires when they become more than 5 years old. Along with weekly inspections, double-check the tires as part of the pre- and post-trip inspections.

Modify Older Vans to Enhance Safety

For older vans, it's important to know that various equipment options can be retrofitted on the vehicles to help improve handling and safety. One option is the installation and conversion to dual rear wheels, which provide a wider, more stable track, lower the van's center of gravity, and greatly reduce the potential for a rear tire failure.

A van's rear suspension can also be upgraded with add-on equipment such as a coil spring stabilizing system for the rear leaf springs or anti-sway bars. Both types of equipment help to reduce body roll and, thus, the risk of vehicle rollover. These types of modifications should be installed by a qualified mechanic or technician who is certified and insured.

Van Safety at a Glance

- Screen all drivers carefully.
- Provide driver training for van operators.
- Do pre- and post-trip inspections of the vehicle, and maintain it regularly.
- Require seat belt use by all passengers.
- Have safety items on board the vehicle (for example, first-aid kit, fire extinguisher).
- Drive conservatively and always under 60 miles per hour.
- Rotate drivers often when on long trips.
- Do not allow drivers to use cell phones when operating the vehicle.
- Do not transport children in 15-passenger vans.
- Consider purchasing a newer van equipped with a stability system. Better yet, purchase a school bus or minibus, which are safer forms of transportation.

Keys to Reducing Rollover Risks

- Use only high-quality, low-mileage tires, and inspect them weekly for proper inflation and tread wear.
- Keep the gas tank as full as possible to lower the vehicle's center of gravity.
- Do not overload the van.
- Never load items on the roof.
- Fill the front seats first, and permanently remove the back seat.
- Do not pull a trailer, and remove the trailer hitch.
- Consider installing dual rear tires on the van to improve stability, or upgrade the suspension.
- Avoid any sudden movement of the steering wheel, rapid maneuvers, and sharp turns, which can result in a chain reaction of overcorrecting and loss of control.

Want a Safer Vehicle?

Consider a multifunction school activity bus (MFSAB). We're not in the business of selling vehicles, but if your church wants one of the safest, most versatile vehicles on the road to transport members, consider purchasing or leasing an MFSAB, also known as a "minibus."

Research shows that school buses are among the safest vehicles. Although MFSABs are not intended to transport children in grades K-12 between home and school, MFSABs are required to meet nearly all of the school bus safety standards, including those for crashworthiness, crash avoidance, and post-crash standards. The only school bus safety features that MFSABs do not have are school bus yellow paint, a stop arm, and flashing lights to control traffic.

In most states, a commercial driver's license (CDL) is not required to operate an MFSAB if there are fewer than 15 passengers, excluding the driver.

A Role Model for Church Transportation

Fellowship Community Church (FCC) in Centennial, Colorado, has a variety of unique transportation needs. For instance, every January and February the youth ministry travels to the Rocky Mountains for winter retreats. On certain Sundays, the children's choir visits nursing homes to sing. A group of home-school students take field trips in the area, and other members travel to events in the community throughout the year.

While there are always risks involved with church-sponsored trips, FCC takes transportation very seriously and has developed a wide variety of policies and procedures to minimize risks and ensure that every journey is as safe as possible.

"About seven years ago, one of the steps we thought was very important to take was eliminating all of our 15-passenger vans," Marie Welch, facilities manager at Fellowship Community Church, commented. "We replaced the vans with two full-size school buses and a 40-passenger people mover—vehicles that are proven to be much safer."

Drivers of the church's vehicles must be at least 25 years of age and are carefully selected and trained. Before people are allowed to drive for the church, they are required to fill out an application form. The application requests information such as the type of license earned, what vehicles they are qualified to operate, addresses for the last five years, descriptions of accidents or traffic violations, and personal insurance coverage.

"Once they've filled out the application, we check their motor vehicle records and do a criminal background search," Welch said. "Basically, we require that all drivers have a clean driving record, no criminal record, and no moving violations in the three previous years." Along with earning a commercial driver's license (CDL) and passenger endorsement, drivers must also complete and pass several training courses.

"For our bus drivers, we have worked out a cooperative agreement with one of the school districts," Welch said. "We allow the district to use our church parking lot to train their bus drivers, and in exchange, they help train our drivers." But for certain trips, drivers are required to gain additional experience.

"We only have a few drivers who are certified to drive our buses in the mountains," Welch noted. "Not only must those drivers pass our screening process, complete initial training, and have the proper licensing, we also require them to get hands-on experience assisting and training with experienced mountain drivers."

Additional transportation safeguards at FCC include regular vehicle maintenance—which is documented—pre- and post-trip inspections, and trip safety procedures for passengers and drivers. Any ministry that wants to use a church vehicle must fill out a request form and have it approved. "We also have incident/accident procedures and forms that drivers are required to use in the event of an accident," Welch said. "Fortunately, though, we haven't had any accidents."

Transportation safety is just one of the many risk management efforts underway at Fellowship Community Church. As an employee of the church for more than eight years and the first woman in America to receive certification in facility management from the National Association of Church Facility Managers, Welch and her team have developed a comprehensive approach to safety and security. It encompasses youth and children's ministry, staff and volunteer safety, financial safeguards, emergency preparedness, and many other areas.

Chapter 10

Additional Risks and Motivation

One of the intentions of this book is to provide your church with a practical reference guide that can be used on an ongoing basis. For instance, as your Church Safety and Security (CSS) Team works through its list of high-priority risks using the EFFECT approach, we hope you'll pick up this book again and refer to the specific chapter that covers the topic on which you're focusing.

Before concluding, though, let's briefly consider four remaining and important issues for churches:

- Allowing Others to Use Your Church
- Hiring Outside Contractors
- Construction Safeguards
- Legal Safeguards and Selecting an Attorney

Allowing Others to Use Your Church

An important question for churches is when, and under what conditions, you should open up your church buildings and property for use by outside groups. Schools, civic associations, other nonprofit organizations, businesses, and even individuals may request to rent or use your church's facility. Consider this experience of a former church administrator:

"One of my more vivid memories as a church administrator was a 'wild animal extravaganza' that took place without our knowledge in our church's family life center. A Cub Scout pack unconnected to the church had rented our facilities for a banquet and as it turned out, arranged for this animal spectacular as the after-dinner entertainment. Standing in the sound room overlooking the banquet, I watched as an animal trainer paraded various wild creatures in front of the young boys below. Visions of newspaper headlines reading 'Bear Escapes at Church' flashed through my head as I worried about all of the terrible things that could happen if something went wrong."

Thankfully, no Cub Scouts were harmed during the wild animal extravaganza. But not all churches are so fortunate when outside groups use their facilities. At another church, for instance, when the local school district was allowed to offer evening classes on church premises, a woman from the community fell while going down the steps. She fractured both ankles, had multiple surgeries, and a permanent disability. Later, she sued the church for negligence and ultimately recovered $550,000.

Legal liabilities aside, there can also be public relations implications when a church rents out its facilities. When the church provides the setting for an event, any incident that occurs can reflect upon the church regardless of its involvement. Imagine what could happen if an outside group holds an event at your church and a child wanders away and is injured, or abused, while the event is going on. Despite the church's lack of participation in the activity, there's a good chance the church's name will be linked with it in subsequent negative media coverage.

Safeguards With Outside Groups

It can be a challenge for a church to balance the desire to be a good neighbor with the risks, time and space demands, and legal liabilities that come with allowing others to use the facility. So how should your church respond? The following are some practical considerations:

1. **Develop a facility usage policy.** The best approach is to develop a facility usage policy in advance that addresses questions such as who will be permitted to rent the facility, the costs, setup and cleanup responsibilities, sales during events, behavioral expectations, and child care arrangements. Also keep in mind that for tax reasons, churches should avoid allowing their premises to be used for political purposes. Similarly, churches need to carefully consider to what extent they will allow their facilities to be rented to for-profit enterprises. Some churches decide to limit rental of their facilities only to groups and events that further the mission and vision of the church.

   A fee schedule should be established that reflects fair rental value of the facilities and addresses related expenses such as maintenance and child care expenses. This schedule may include a security deposit to protect against property damage. Responsibility for setup and cleanup of the facility needs to be determined before the event. Sales of goods or wares at events on church premises raise tax considerations that should be addressed with the church's tax attorney or accountant before being permitted. The policy should address behavioral issues such as the church's expectations regarding drinking, smoking, participants' conduct, and treating the property with care. Last, consider child care arrangements for outside events. Some churches require that the group use (and pay for) child care providers screened and selected by the church, while others allow the group to make their own child care arrangements. There are pros and cons to each approach.

2. **Document facility usage requests.** With the church's policy in place, a simple facility request form should be used to gather details about the event, obtain contact information, and document the process. Many churches require a member to "sponsor" an outside group. For groups unknown to the church, references from places where the group has held events in the past should be requested and checked.

3. **Maintain an approval process.** Put a mechanism in place for church leadership to approve or deny facility usage requests from outside groups. Approval from a body or team rather than a single individual provides a broader perspective on the event and addresses how the event relates to the church's mission as well as competing facility concerns. Informal uses of the building that are not disclosed to church leaders can have significant safety, liability, tax, or financial consequences and should be prohibited. Keep documentation of approval or denial of all requests.

4. **Use a facility usage agreement.** Once the group has been approved, confirm the event in writing, and have the group sign a facility usage agreement. The purpose of the agreement is fourfold: It will confirm the costs involved, specify the times the facility will be available to the group, and set out your church's expectations for the group's use of the facilities. But most important, the agreement will provide protection for the church by including a release from liability and a "hold harmless clause" in which the outside group agrees to indemnify the church for any injuries or damages that may occur while they are using the church. A sample "Church/Facilities Usage and Hold Harmless Agreement" can be found in the *SafeChurch Resource Packet* (free for download at www.safechurch.com). Whatever agreement you use, we recommend that an attorney review it to make sure it complies with local laws.

5. **Make sure outside groups are insured.** When an outside group uses the church's facility, there's no reason to put your church's insurance claims history—and potentially your insurance premiums—on the line. The other group's insurance, not yours, should be at risk. To do this, check that the group has sufficient insurance coverage limits, and require it to name the church as an additional insured on its insurance policies. Then have the group provide proof it has done so. A certificate of insurance that lists your church as an additional insured (not just as a "certificate holder") or, better, an endorsement (change) to the group's policy naming the church as an additional insured is evidence of insurance.

Sometimes the user simply will not have insurance. In that situation, the church has two options: (1) Require the group to obtain insurance or (2) allow the group to use the church anyway. While the first option sounds difficult, a couple of alternatives are available. First, the group may check with one or more of its homeowners' insurers to see if the group can obtain a certificate of liability insurance covering the church. Note, however, that most homeowners insurance policy liability limits are low. Second, there are special markets for obtaining one-time liability insurance for private events such as weddings and banquets. For example, for a modest one-time charge, the group can usually obtain $1 million in liability insurance coverage that also names the church as an additional insured. The church is free to require outside users to carry such insurance. A careful cost-benefit ministry analysis should be undertaken before deciding to allow an uninsured group to rent the facilities.

In the end, the decision to deny a facility request or to require items such as a facility usage agreement or proof of insurance can be an uncomfortable one for a church. Still, it's better for the church to be prepared on the front end than to be surprised on the back end.

Hiring Outside Contractors

As discussed earlier in this book, repairs to your church may call for the use of outside contractors. But without carefully selecting the contractor and taking steps to ensure that the church is protected, your church may be exposed to additional damage or liability stemming from the actions of contractors. Here are two real-life examples:

A historic church in Illinois was in need of roof repair. It obtained several estimates and hired the contractor that provided the lowest bid. However, the church did not check the contractor's references and later discovered there had been several complaints from other customers. While working on the project at the historic church, the contractor's employees accidentally set the building's roof on fire. According to a newspaper report, when the employees realized what they had done, "they gathered their tools and went home." The historic church was completely destroyed in the blaze.

In New York, a synagogue hired a contractor to renovate its facilities. There was no written contract between the temple and the contractor. The work involved the use of a scaffold, but no safety harness or scaffold railings were provided. One of the contractor's employees fell from the scaffolding to the ground below, suffering debilitating leg injuries that resulted in six surgeries. The worker sued the contractor and the synagogue, obtaining a settlement in excess of $1 million, including over $500,000 from the synagogue.

Selecting a Contractor

The first step in the selection of a contractor is to check the contractor's references. Contact other businesses or, ideally, other churches where the contractor has performed work and see if they had any issues or problems. Contact the Better Business Bureau or your local chamber of commerce to determine if any complaints have been filed against the company. Next, determine whether the contractor carries appropriate insurance for the job including general liability, property, workers' compensation, and umbrella (excess) insurance.

Once an agreement has been reached on the scope of the work and its cost, use a written contract for the work. While it is recommended that the church's attorney review such contracts, there are two provisions that are especially important to include: (1) a hold harmless clause in which the contractor agrees to indemnify, or hold harmless, the church from any damage or injury that the contractor might cause in performing the job and (2) an additional insurance provision in which the contractor agrees to add the church as an "additional insured" on the contractor's insurance policies. This will ensure that the contractor's insurance coverage and rates are at risk during the job, not the church's.

Make sure to follow through and have the contractor supply proof that your church has been added as an additional insured on his or her policies. A "certificate of insurance" is some evidence of coverage, but make sure the church is listed on the certificate as an additional insured (not just as a "certificate holder"). Also, contact the insurance company to verify that your church has been added as an additional insured. Even better, obtain an "additional insured endorsement" from the contractor's insurance company that shows your church is an additional insured on the contractor's policies.

Finally, avoid paying for the entire job upfront. Rather, work out a payment schedule with final payment due after the work has been completed to your church's satisfaction.

Construction Safeguards

According to the McGraw-Hill Dodge Market Report, approximately $4 billion is spent in religious building construction each year as thousands of churches undertake construction projects. The financial and "people" risks involved in such large projects warrant special consideration by churches. What many churches do not fully appreciate is that safety should begin in the design phase, not after the ground is broken and construction is underway. Before finalizing their building design, churches should talk to their architect about safety considerations such as those shown below.

Safety Considerations in Designing a New Building

- Programmable keyless entry into the building to avoid "key control" issues
- Front office/reception area security through design
- Crime prevention through environmental design techniques including exterior lighting and appropriate landscaping
- Security system and video surveillance cameras
- Centralized registration area for children's ministry
- High visibility (glass) in children's and youth areas
- Children/youth ministry restroom design that avoids the use of restroom doors
- Greater visibility such as doors with glass panels for pastors' offices and counseling areas
- Avoiding "nooks and crannies" where unobserved activity can take place
- Conductor and grounding system with surge protection against lightning and transient voltage surges
- Evacuation route planning, signage, and emergency lighting
- Interior shelter room(s) to take cover in during a severe thunderstorm or tornado warning
- Central station fire alarm and sprinkler system
- Automatic water leak detection and/or shut-off capability
- Facility access for the elderly and disabled
- Sufficient storage space to avoid storing materials in mechanical and boiler rooms

Addressing safety issues in the design stage can save a lot of time and expense in retrofitting the church for safety down the road. Your church may also want to discuss these issues with your insurance agent, other safety professionals, and your local law enforcement and fire departments before your design plans are complete.

Make sure to also discuss "builder's risk" insurance with your insurance agent or broker. This insurance covers new construction until the building is completed. You want to make sure that the new building is not left uninsured while it is being built. Once the building is complete, make sure that your agent or broker adds the new building to your insurance policy, ideally on a replacement cost basis.

The steps mentioned in the preceding section, "Hiring Outside Contractors," are just as applicable in selecting a construction contractor. Specifically, check references, make sure the contract is in writing and includes indemnification and additional insurance provisions, obtain proof that the church has been added as an additional insured on the contractor's insurance policies, and work out an agreeable payment schedule.

In addition, churches need to be aware of what are known in the law as "materialman's" or "mechanic's" liens. These are liens that suppliers of construction materials can assert against the building itself until they are paid. If a contractor fails to make payment for construction materials, the supplier can institute a process to force the sale of the property to satisfy the lien unless the property owner (the church) makes payment itself. To avoid this situation, churches should insist upon "lien waivers" from all suppliers involved in the project and include a lien waiver requirement in the construction contract. As you can imagine, given the complexity and risk involved in construction projects, consultation with a competent attorney is essential.

While (for financial reasons) churches may be tempted to serve as their own contractor or build the structure themselves with volunteer labor, the risks that go along with such an approach can easily overshadow the money savings. The stories of improper building construction or, worse, injury or even death to volunteers working on church building projects are heartbreaking and disturbingly common. For example, a volunteer working alone on the renovation of a church's worship space fell from a ladder onto the concrete below. He died from the head injuries he received.

During the time that construction is ongoing at your church, take steps to keep your congregation safe. The construction zone should be fenced or roped off so that no one, especially children, gains unauthorized access. (See the concluding example in this chapter.) Access to the building project should be scheduled only with the general contractor's permission and only if it is safe to do so. Hard hats and appropriate footwear should be required. Any changes to regular walkways caused by the construction project should be inspected to make sure they remain safe. Finally, no part of the new building should be occupied until the responsible local government agency has inspected the property and issued an occupancy permit.

Legal Safeguards and Selecting an Attorney

A good number of the subjects addressed in this book have touched upon legal issues. It is an unfortunate reality in today's world that every church needs to have available to it the counsel of an experienced attorney.

Legal Matters

Some of the legal issues facing churches today that are best addressed by consultation with legal counsel include the following:

- organizational structure and governing documents such as the church constitution, articles of incorporation, and bylaws
- federal tax-exempt status
- state and local property, income, and sales tax exemptions
- church discipline of members
- employment practices and disputes
- compliance with copyright laws
- establishing a preschool, day care, or school
- construction or renovation projects
- application of privacy rules and HIPAA to church documents, publications, and websites
- liabilities and immunities of board members
- zoning, land use, and property disputes

(This is an overview of the most frequent topics for which legal consultation is advised, not a complete list of the legal issues that can arise in the ministry of a church.)

So how do you go about selecting an attorney for the church? Very often, an attorney is selected by default when church leaders learn that a congregation member, or the relative of one, is a lawyer. But legal practice today has become more specialized than in the past. The law affecting nonprofit organizations and, specifically, churches, is unique and requires an in-depth understanding, especially as it relates to the First Amendment. In selecting the church's attorney, consider the following:

1. Ask for references from the attorney and, specifically, references from religious institutions or other nonprofit organizations the attorney has served in the past. Select an attorney who is familiar with the way churches operate and who understands your language.
2. Investigate the lawyer's background. Contact the state and local bar associations and the local court system to determine whether any complaints or judgments have been filed against the lawyer. You do not want an attorney who has been found guilty of misconduct by the bar or the court.
3. Ask about the attorney's knowledge and experience with the laws affecting nonprofit and religious organizations. You should feel completely comfortable with the person's understanding of the law in this area before retaining him or her.
4. Negotiate the fees that will be charged, and reduce your agreement to writing so there is no confusion. Many attorneys will provide reduced rates or even pro bono (no charge) services to nonprofit religious organizations such as churches.
5. If you're part of a denomination, ask the state or local denominational office who provides its legal services. An attorney familiar with your denominational structure is a bonus, both in terms of knowledge of church law and potential willingness to provide discounted legal services to a local church associated with a denominational client.

With these steps, your church will be in a better position to secure competent legal counsel who will be able to advise you on the many legal pitfalls facing churches today.

Of course, not every risk that a church might face has been addressed in these pages. So we encourage you to review the *SafeChurch Resource Packet* (free for download at www.safechurch.com), which provides information on additional subjects such as violence at church, kitchen safeguards, practicing church discipline, and computer and Internet safety.

Conclusion

One Sunday morning in November, nobody in the sanctuary at Cornerstone Faith[1] imagined that a little girl would be seriously injured nearby while the pastor finished the worship service.

Earlier that year, the church had set out to build a new family life center next to its main facility. In an effort to control construction costs, the church decided to act

[1] This incident actually occurred, but the names have been changed to protect privacy.

as its own general contractor on the expansion project. Gradually, as construction work proceeded, the new center was taking shape.

On the day of the accident, Sunday school classes had ended before the worship service, and several teachers took a group of kids outside to play. Despite the ongoing construction, the new center's structure was not locked or secured in any way. At some point, an 11-year-old girl, Samantha, wandered unnoticed into the building. She climbed to the second floor and accidentally fell, landing on the concrete slab below.

Later, when Samantha could not be found, she was discovered in the construction area lying unconscious, with serious head injuries. After being rushed to the hospital, Samantha was in a coma for several weeks, underwent two brain surgeries, and spent one month in the hospital.

The medical and rehabilitation bills for Samantha's care cost several hundred thousand dollars. Her family eventually brought a claim against the church for negligence alleging the dangerous condition of its facilities and the lack of supervision over the Sunday school class.

Costs on Many Levels

We're pleased to report that Samantha recovered from her injuries. But the outcome could have been much worse.

As a tragedy that should have been prevented, the story illustrates how an unfortunate incident can impact a church, its members, and its leaders on many different levels. Could your church experience a similar nightmare? Consider the following real and potential "costs" of such an accident:

The health and safety of members—Someone at the church should have recognized the dangers of the construction project and made sure the area was secure. And why were children allowed to be near the construction site and not properly supervised? As a result, Samantha's health and safety were sacrificed, and other children were put at risk.

Physical and emotional trauma—In addition to Samantha's parents, every member of the church was heartbroken after the accident. Leaders were grief-stricken, and the woman supervising Samantha's class faces a lifetime of guilt.

Anger and resentment—Rightfully so, Samantha's parents were angry when they learned that nothing had been done to secure the construction area. And because a beloved member of the congregation was not properly supervised, other members of the church were angry as well.

Though not present in Samantha's case, the following additional costs are often incurred when something goes awry at church. (These costs are especially common in incidents of child sexual abuse at church.)

Damage to the ministry—An accident or incident can cause members to lose confidence in the church. Members may worry that their children aren't safe or may be at risk. It can take years to repair this damage. Some churches never recover and are forced to close their doors.

Loss of membership—A serious incident, such as one involving misconduct by the pastor or other key staff, can cause members to stop attending the church.

Loss of giving—With the loss of members goes a loss of their tithes and offerings.

Adverse publicity—Media attention that focuses on an accident or incident can tarnish the church's reputation in the community. For a period of time, it may become difficult to recruit new members because of the adverse publicity.

Questioning of pastoral leadership—When an accident or incident occurs, some people may have hard questions for church leaders, such as, Why didn't they prevent it? What was their involvement? Was the response appropriate? Consequently, the pastors' leadership or decision-making abilities may be called into question.

A costly lawsuit—A lawsuit stemming from an accident or incident is an unpleasant situation for church leaders as they must relive the incident, defend the allegations against them, engage in expensive and emotional litigation, and face the financial consequences of a lawsuit, all while trying to maintain unity and continuing to minister to the congregation.

So Much at Stake

Samantha's fall at the construction site is just one more example of the thousands of needless accidents and other incidents that occur at churches each year. And depending on the severity and nature of the situation, the costs—be they emotional, ministerial, or monetary—are frequently much greater.

Since many of these incidents could have been prevented, it's hard to understand why more church leaders are not focusing on safety and security today. Fortunately, though, you understand exactly what's at stake and are ready to launch or strengthen your church's risk management ministry.

The Inspiration to Act Now

If you've been reading this book, we know you are passionate about safeguarding people, church property, and other precious resources. So your next mission will be to inspire others at your church to join you in creating a ministry of safety and security.

Overall, the goal will be to address church risk management through a comprehensive, well-thought-out program that seeks to preserve ministry, keeps God's people safe, and secures the resources of the church. When you're communicating this idea to others at your church, it may be helpful to focus on three basic concepts that recap our discussions to this point: value, team, and work.

Value—While the fear of legal claims and lawsuits against the church may motivate some people to action, a more positive approach is to focus on the spiritual values of shepherding, stewardship, and love.

Church leaders are called to be shepherds of their congregations. One aspect of shepherding is to protect the flock against wolves (hazards) that may cause harm. Church leaders are also called to be good stewards of the people and property entrusted to them.

Finally, by showing concern for the safety and security of your congregation, you are expressing love to one another. By focusing on the values of shepherding, stewardship, and love, you can encourage and motivate others to embrace safety and security within your congregation.

Team—Create a Church Safety and Security (CSS) Team that is passionate about protecting people and church resources. This team will focus on risk management and should include congregation members who educate themselves and other members of the church on safety and security issues facing the organization.

By identifying members of the church whose jobs or special interests relate to safety and risk management—in fields such as facility or property management, human resources, law, accounting, law enforcement, insurance, or safety—a committed group of members can successfully run the risk management program. While pastoral or board participation on the team is not essential, support from church leaders is crucial to the team's success.

Work—Encourage the CSS Team to get to work identifying areas of risk (using the "EFFECT" approach) and taking steps to address those risks. Yet by no means does the team need to work alone in this effort. A wealth of resources—including assessment tools, training, checklists, forms, sample policies, and procedures—are available online in the *SafeChurch Resource Packet* (free for download at www .safechurch.com). The many resources on this site are designed to provide you and your CSS Team with just about everything you need to build a risk management program from scratch.

Let the Ministry Begin

Creating a risk management ministry is much like a church mission to a foreign country. The journey requires research, preparation, and planning before you go. Once the mission is underway, there's work to do and there are challenges to overcome. Each member of the mission brings his or her own talents. And together, you do the Lord's work and pray for strength. At the end of the day, you can look back on what has been accomplished, knowing that you've made a difference and perhaps even saved a life. As King David expressed it, "Trust in the Lord and do good; dwell in the land and enjoy safe pasture" (Psalm 37:3).

Index

Topics covered in the *SafeChurch Resource Packet* are referenced by document number rather than page number and are preceded by SCRP.

Volunteers need more than punch and cookies.

Multiplying Ministry From Me to We

Invite. Equip. Retain. Lead. Protect.

Get a taste of the good stuff with Church Volunteer Central.
A membership gives you all the ingredients for finding,
growing, and keeping great volunteers.
Expand your ministry. Lighten your load. Calories optional.

Start today at www.ChurchVolunteerCentral.com

Church Volunteer Central®

Incredible things will happen™

800-761-2095

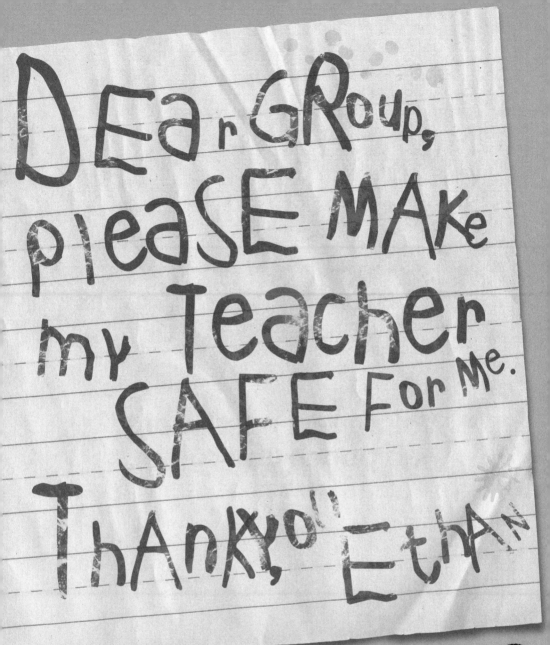

Shepherd's Watch™ Background Checks

SHEPHERD'S
WATCH
Background Checks
Trusted service. Superior support.

Give Ethan the protection he deserves.
It's easy. Church Volunteer Central has expanded its services and support to provide quick, thorough background checks for your church. Contact us and we'll help you take good care of your ministry, your volunteers, and Ethan.

Visit www.ChurchVolunteerCentral.com

Group
Incredible things will happen™

group.com • 800-761-2095

Discover...

Simply Strategic Stuff

Help for Leaders Drowning in the Details of Running a Church

Tim Stevens and Tony Morgan

Easy-to-understand and humorous, *Simply Strategic Stuff* covers 99 topics church leaders need to know to perform the administrative details of pastoring with ease—and enthusiasm.

ISBN 978-0-7644-2625-4

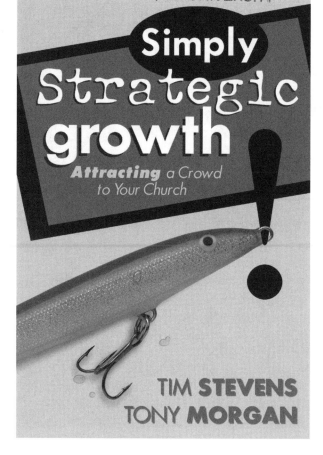

Discover...

Simply Strategic Growth
Attracting a Crowd to Your Church
Tim Stevens and Tony Morgan

This great resource will help with the practical and creative sides of planning church services. Includes advice on facilities, parking, church environment, children's ministry, promotion, programming, and philosophy.

ISBN 978-0-7644-2865-4